What others are saying

"I thoroughly enjoyed reading The Up and Up on Parenting! Ms Peterson's book is insightful, humorous, and intuitive. It is written in a way that every parent can relate to, full of real-life and practical examples, and understandable instruction. Thank you for understanding children, behavior, and relationships so well and for sharing your knowledge with the rest of us!"

—Valerie Hoffer MA, Licensed Mental Health Counselor

"I found this book to be a refreshing change in contrast to so many self-help books written in terms that don't feel relatable to the everyday challenges of parenting. The real-life scenarios and thought-provoking questions were extremely helpful in providing guidance and hope, making the experience of reading this book, both personal and rewarding."

—Sandy O'Brien, RN, MN, ACM, CL

"What I enjoyed most about reading 'The Up and Up on Parenting' was the simple yet powerful instruction on how to handle everyday parenting questions. Using time-honored parenting techniques, Geralyn writes in a way that is easy to follow with substantial redirection that brings hope to those facing difficult behaviors. Each section was a pleasure to read and reflect on."

—Kara Meyer, MS, LMHC, CMHS

"Parenting is a great challenge; the Up and Up on Parenting reminds us that it is also a joy and an adventure. With her clear concepts, relatable examples and practical exercises, Ms. Peterson helps parents understand and apply skills and strategies that help their children be and become their best selves. After reading this optimistic and constructive book, you will find your skill, your confidence, and your joy in parenting go up, and up and up."

—Patrick Snow, Publishing Coach, Bestselling Author *Creating Your Own Destiny*

"Every Pediatrician and Family Counselor should read this book twice, and recommend it as a resource to families of all ages. The practical exercises allow the parent and child to engage in the solution. The Author debuts a witty, clever guide, blazing a new trail along our parenting paths. I was laughing so much, at my "mistakes," knowing I could use them as learning opportunities for my children and me! Move over "What to.." there's a new Best Parenting Book on the shelf!"

—Maryjane C., BA, M.A.S. Criminology , Law and Society

"Geralyn Peterson teaches us that our children's mistakes are opportunities for us to teach them and opportunities for them to learn. Get ready, because this book is an excellent guide, and I am sure that you will teach your kid without feeling guilty.

"The Up And Up On Parenting contains several explanations that can help us be positive while teaching and stop those sometimes embarrassing moments when our kid has a tantrum. Do they listen to you when you are lecturing them? Do they do what they are told? Expect to learn parenting concepts and skills through examples that will help teach them. You will be able to read examples and do exercises to help understand these concepts and skills. I recommend this book as it is inspiring and well written. You can expect thorough explanations that aim to help the reader to solve his daily issues.

I enjoyed how Geralyn keeps encouraging us to move on and be positive. Negative words attract negativity, so let us cut those words from our vocabulary! It is a breath of fresh air!"

—Reprospace Editorial Reviews™

"I loved this book! As a parent, this is a book I wish I would have read when my kids were still kids! As an educator, this is a book I'm glad I read now. The strategies and solutions provided by this thought provoking and entertaining book can be applied to both parents and teachers. Children certainly don't come with a "how to" manual, and parenting indeed is one of the hardest jobs in the world. Ms. Peterson fills her book with real life scenarios that ring true. The suggestions she offers us gave me more than one "Aha" moment, even though my oldest child is now 35 years old and I've been an educator for 24+ years! Filled with pertinent quotations, antidotes, exercises to deepen your thinking, and spot on advice, this book is a must read for any parent or teacher who seeks to fully understand effective and thoughtful strategies to teach life lessons to young people. I came away from this book refreshed, hopeful, and eager to try some of these strategies with my students and my grandchildren. Not only does Ms. Peterson cover a myriad of situations that come up frequently in a course of a normal life, she delves into the how and the why of human behavior a lot deeper than many books or discipline programs dare to go. Highly recommended!"

—Wayne Osborn, National Board Certified Teacher, M.Ed, M.L.I.S.

"As parents, it can be tough to sort through the myriad of suggestions and advice out there. "The Up and Up on Parenting" is a wonderful tool in that it invites self-reflection and incorporates exercises that help you to understand where your parenting choices come from and encourages you to try different, more effective methods. I highly recommend this book as it is a thought-provoking and informative resource that will definitely change the way you look at the many challenges and rewards of parenting."

—Jennifer Dye, MBA, CBA

"Many of the struggles we have with the boys is our lack of structure. Bedtime is riddled with distractions. Our patience gets frayed trying to keep the boys focused. "The Up and Up on Parenting" has taught me to say, "I like that you're coming up with all these ideas, but you still need to get your pajamas on." Or to calmly respond to every "But I just gotta…," with the simple word, "Pajamas." We are making progress by building predicab structure into our home. Thank you for the positive influence you have had on our lives!"

—Venessa L Walker, MA Science Education

"The Up and Up on Parenting really challenged my thinking surrounding discipline in the classroom. As a high school teacher, it can be easy to react impulsively and emotionally to a student who is misbehaving. As a result, the fragile relationships that I have with my students can be harmed. Ms. Peterson's book inspired me to reconsider how I approach student misbehavior. I am equipped with new tools, strategies, and a more positive mindset surrounding student consequences."

—Rachel Pack, M. Ed.

Up & Up PARENTING

Reframing your Children's
Mistakes as Teaching Moments

Geralyn Peterson, LMHC

The Up and Up on Parenting: Reframing your Children's Mistakes as Teaching Moments

First edition, published 2021

By Geralyn Peterson

Editors: Larry Alexander and Tyler Tichelaar, Superior Book Productions

Cover Design: Haley Chriswell

Interior Book by Design: Reprospace, LLC

ISBN Softcover: 978-1-952685-24-8

Every attempt has been made to source properly all quotes.

Published by Kitsap Publishing, www.KitsapPublishing.com

Printed in the United States of America

Dedication

To my daughter, who challenged me, delighted me and taught me.

And still does.

Acknowledgments

I have so many people who have helped me by supporting my journey, shaping my ideas, and constructing this book. Thank you to all the parents and clients who shared their parenting journey with me. A special thanks to Emerald Peterson, Venessa Walker, Wayne Osborn, Anna Fryer, Rachel Pack, Patricia Deter Baum, Mike Baum, Cindy Dout, Lori Escobar, Patrick Snow, Karla Kluge, Laura Johnson, Marge Steckler, Sandy Obrien, Valerie Hoffer, Tyler Tichelaar, Ingemar Anderson, William Asher, Haley Criswell

Contents

Introduction

*"There can be no keener revelation of a society's soul than
the way in which it treats its children."*
—Nelson Mandela

The mistakes your children make are opportunities for you to teach them, and opportunities for them to learn. Mistakes can teach lessons that no lecture, punishment, or reward can teach. The more mistakes children make, the fewer they will make as adults. Parenting well is the ability to use the mistakes your children make to teach them lessons you want them to learn.

"Tell me and I forget. Teach me and I remember. Involve me and I learn."
—Benjamin Franklin

When you lecture, do your children listen, or do they tune you out? When you spank, do your children learn what not to do, or how not to get caught doing it? When you ground your children, do they spend that time feeling remorse, or do they spend it feeling angry at you for punishing them? How often do you step in and stop your children from making a mistake before they can experience the consequences of their actions and learn from them? And when they do make mistakes, how often do you use those mistakes as opportunities to teach responsibility, honesty, optimism, confidence, tolerance, and empathy? If you punish too soon, your child does not have time to reflect on their own behavior and they miss the opportunity to learn from their mistakes. You lose the opportunity to teach them how to fix their mistakes and not make the same ones again. When you allow your children to make mistakes, you can teach them all you want them to learn.

Parenting is one of the most difficult—and most important—jobs in the world. In high school, we are taught algebra, geography, and chemistry, but few of us are taught parenting. Since most of us will become parents, most of us are in more need of parenting skills than trigonometry.

In this book, you will learn many parenting concepts and skills to help your children learn the things you want to teach them. I will share examples to help you understand these concepts and skills. And you will complete exercises to solidify the concepts and skills so they become comfortable and even effortless. You will learn the value of mistakes and how to guide your child through the lessons their mistakes bring. You will learn the importance of listening to feelings, while not letting your empathy and understanding interfere with consequences. You will learn to teach consequences that truly help your child learn and internalize lessons. You will learn how to praise your child in a way that allows them to admire and appreciate their own abilities and appreciate you as a parent. You will learn how to raise successful children.

"It is easier to build strong children than to repair broken men."
—Frederick Douglass

Foreword

No one book can provide all you need to become a better parent. This book offers many ideas and skills, but the actual list of helpful ideas and skills is endless. Children are constantly changing, parents are constantly changing, and the world is constantly changing. A strategy that works with one child may not work with another. A technique that works today may not work tomorrow. Our parenting skills should also evolve.

Raising children is an ever-changing adventure. But it is a rewarding adventure, and it can be an enjoyable one. By reading this book, parents can learn valuable skills and leave behind frustrating practices. I hope parents will learn to become their children's teachers rather than their children's punisher. By understanding this book, parents will learn to use positive feedback to help their children continue positive behavior. I know most parents are ready to help their children be all they can be. Now parents will have the skills to enjoy parenting while raising happy, healthy, successful and kind adults.

Geralyn Peterson is a Licensed Mental Health Counselor and Supervisor. She is a child mental health specialist with over 20 years of experience providing child and family counseling, education, and parenting classes. Mrs. Peterson also teaches courses on talking to your kids and parenting children exposed to domestic violence. Her book is based on the program "The Up and Up on Parenting," which she developed and uses in her private practice.

Her experience ranges from crisis mental health, community mental health, and private practice. Geralyn believes in a holistic approach to therapy, addressing emotional, mental, physical, and spiritual well-being as it impacts choices and behavior. She understands the impact of each person's environment, including family, culture, and society. Her goal is to help every person envision themselves as the best version of themselves and make the changes that help them attain that vision.

Her belief, as well as her experience in teaching, consultation, crisis intervention, and a Master of Arts from Chapman University in Psychology with a child, family, and marriage emphasis, helped her raise me, her 'Perfect Daugther,' addressing her well-being, challenges, and growth. She believes that parenting well means using mistakes as opportunities to teach your children lessons. Since my mother and I both made mistakes, she was inspired to write this book and share the perspective that every mistake is a teaching and learning opportunity.

—Emerald Peterson, Daughter of the Author

1

Mistakes

Spilled juice and Newton's apple

"A life spent making mistakes is not only more honorable, but more useful than a life spent doing nothing."

—George Bernard Shaw

Most of us think of mistakes as something to avoid. Before inventing the light bulb, Thomas Edison "failed" to invent it many, many times. He made mistake after mistake after mistake. Instead of viewing those experiments as mistakes, he viewed them as significant successes.

When asked, "Mr. Edison, how did it feel to fail (to invent the light bulb) 999 times?" Edison smiled and replied, "Young man, I have not failed 999 times. I have simply found 999 ways how not to create a light bulb."

Thomas Edison believed in making mistakes. While Edison is known for inventing the light bulb, I believe his greater contribution may have been his perspective on mistakes. He also said, "The most certain way to succeed is always to try just one more time."

Edison believed mistakes were essential on the road to success. Making mistakes means you are trying to learn. They shouldn't be avoided; rather, they should be celebrated, because mistakes bring us closer to success.

Write down something difficult you tried but gave up on that you wish you had kept trying to do even though you were afraid of failing:

_____

_____

Think of something difficult your child is doing that they want to give up because they are afraid they might fail:

Think of something you are encouraging your child to continue to do, even though they have become frustrated with the mistakes they have made:

_____

_____

If Thomas Edison, often called "America's greatest inventor," made mistakes, it's pretty likely your children will make mistakes, too.

Not only will your children inevitably make mistakes, ~~but~~ it is important to allow them to do so. Mistakes will help them learn. Falling is what helps toddlers learn to walk, and what helps kids learn to ride a bicycle. Toddlers can learn the mechanics of walking in a baby walker, but since the walker prevents them from falling down, it takes toddlers who use walkers longer to learn to walk. It takes them longer to learn balance. While it may seem safer to put your child in a walker, it's actually safer to help them learn balance. If kids are not given the opportunity to fall, it is harder for them to learn to walk. If kids aren't given the opportunity to make mistakes, it is harder for them to learn.

> *"A parent's job isn't to prevent their children from falling,*
> *but to pick them up when they do."*
>
> **—Aaron DeCamp**

The mistakes children make are opportunities to teach. Understanding and evaluating mistakes helps them learn. Helping your child understand and evaluate their mistakes is part of being a parent. You can be patient with your child when they make a mistake. You can be understanding. You can even be grateful. Every mistake they make when they are younger is one less mistake they are likely to make when they are older and the consequences are greater.

Be patient with repeated mistakes. Repeated mistakes reinforce the lessons your children are learning.

When Veronica's daughter, Sutton, was about six, she wanted some juice but could not figure out how to open the juice box. She came up with the creative solution of cutting a hole in the bottom. Of course, juice spilled out all over the kitchen floor in a sticky mess. As Veronica and Sutton cleaned up the juice together, they had a wonderful discussion about how Newton "discovered" gravity when an apple fell on his head and how Galileo experimented with how fast objects fall. Sutton was a scientist just like Newton and Galileo. She discovered juice will run out of the bottom of a juice box if you cut a hole in it. She "discovered" gravity. Sutton's mistake not only gave Veronica a wonderful opportunity to teach, but it gave her daughter confidence and gave them both a wonderful opportunity to bond. Veronica did talk to Sutton about asking an adult for help when using a sharp knife. She also showed Sutton how to open a juice box. And Sutton did have to clean up the juice she spilled. By focusing on the "mistake" of opening a juice box at the bottom, Sutton began to think of herself as a scientist. Because of this mistake, Sutton's knowledge increased (she learned how to open a juice box), her confidence increased (she began to think of herself as a scientist), her trust in her mother increased (she realized her mother knew the proper way to open a juice box), and her relationship with her mother strengthened (she had a pleasant and inspiring conversation with her mother). All of these are important. Perhaps the least important of these is learning how to open a juice box. Arguably, the most important is strengthening the relationship between Sutton and her mother. Because of that experience, Sutton will feel more comfortable sharing and discussing mistakes with her mother.

If a child isn't given the freedom to fall, they aren't as quick to learn to walk. If a child isn't given the freedom to make a mess in their high chair, they will be slower to learn to manage a spoon and fork. If a child isn't given the freedom to be cold, they won't listen to you when you tell them to bring a coat to school. Mistakes teach us specific things, and also deeper lessons about responsibility, organization, empathy, cause and effect, etc.

Let's look at some examples. Think about each situation and fill in your ideas.

Example 1:

A child makes the mistake of throwing a toy when they are angry:

The simple lesson is about _____

The deeper lesson is about _____

If they aren't allowed to make that mistake, as an adult they might _____

Example 2:

A child makes the mistake of leaving wet towels on the floor:

The simple lesson is about _____

The deeper lesson is about _____

If they aren't allowed to make that mistake, as an adult they might _____

Example 3:

A child makes the mistake of not filling up the car with gas after using it:

The simple lesson is about _____

The deeper lesson is about _____

If they aren't allowed to make that mistake, as an adult they might _____

Now let's review.

Example 1:

For throwing a toy when they are angry, the simple lesson is about not throwing things; the deeper lesson is about empathy, anger management, and the difference between emotions and actions. If a child isn't allowed to make this mistake and learn from it, as an adult they might "blow up" at family members, hurt others when they feel angry, or experience depression from ignoring their feelings if they don't know how to helpfully address them.

Example 2:

For wet towels on the floor, the simple lesson is about germs, hygiene, and sharing chores; the deeper lesson is about responsibility, thinking ahead, and consequences. If a child isn't allowed to make this mistake and learn from it, as an adult, they might ignore warning lights in their car, not pay bills until it is too late, or get fired because coworkers had to pick up their slack.

Example 3:

For leaving an empty gas tank, the simple lesson is about fueling a car; the deeper lesson is about planning ahead, thinking of others, and preventative care. If a child isn't allowed to make this mistake and learn from it, as an adult, they might avoid going to the dentist, be selfish in relationships, or, yes, run out of gas.

If your child makes the mistake of stealing when they are six years old, you can address it more easily than if they steal as a teenager or an adult. If your child fails to turn in their homework in fourth grade, you can address it much more easily than if they don't turn in homework in high school. Addressing it in fourth grade might help them turn in homework in high school or might prevent them from being fired for irresponsibility as an adult.

It is important to allow our children to make mistakes. It is also important to guide them before and after they make a mistake. They still need guidance even if they've learned from their mistake; perhaps you can use the mistake they made in one situation and ask them how they can apply it to other situations. To teach them to ride a bike, you create a safe environment, provide encouragement, show them how to ride, explain how to ride, ride with them, and give them opportunities to practice. And then you allow them the opportunity to make the mistake of falling. You also talk to them afterward to help them learn. You can talk to them about why they fell; maybe they fell because they hit a large rock, or because they weren't paying attention, or because they were riding too fast. You can talk to them about what they might do differently next time. Also, you pick them up, comfort them, and encourage them after a fall.

> *"There are two ways to keep a child from drowning:*
> *never let them near the water or teach them how to swim."*
>
> **—Unknown**

Letting a child have their own experiences works better than warning, explaining, lecturing, or limiting them. Allowing them the space to make mistakes is more helpful.

Think of examples of things you didn't learn when they were explained to you, but you did learn when you did them for yourself:

_____

_____

_____

_____

Think of things you do for your child because it is easier than taking the time to let them learn to do it them for themselves:

_____

_____

_____

_____

"I think that the best thing we can do for our children is to allow them to do things for them-selves, allow them to be strong, allow them to experience life on their own terms...let them be better people, let them believe more in themselves."

—C. Joybell C.

It's okay, and even responsible, to remind your child of the possible consequences of their mistakes. A good baseline is to caution them no more than three times. After that, they will either tune you out or think you are trying to control their lives rather than on your message. When kids make a mistake after we have cautioned them, not only do they learn the lesson, but they also learn that their parents might actually know a thing or two. Maybe they'll listen to us next time. Maybe they'll listen to us in more serious situations. Wouldn't it be nice if your child thought you were really, really smart? If that appeals to you, instead of lecturing and protecting your child from bad decisions, caution them once or twice; then let them see for themselves how smart you are!

"Creativity is allowing yourself to make mistakes.
Art is knowing which ones to keep."

—Scott Adams

The lessons from some mistakes are obvious; in that case, just let your child draw their own conclusions. The lessons from other mistakes might be more difficult to figure out. When discussing it with them, let them talk first, giving them the opportunity to figure out what they could have done differently. If they can't figure it out, let them know your thoughts in one minute or less. (If you can't say it in a minute, it's probably too complicated for them to grasp. And after a minute, they will tune you out, anyway.) Say, "When you did A, the result was B. What could you do differently next time?" The idea is simply to repeat the sequence of events. "When you cut the box of juice, the juice all spilled on the floor. How can you get juice next time?" "When you didn't study, you got a 'D'. How can you prepare better next time?" If they can't come up with any ideas, or don't know what to do differently, you can absolutely give them ideas: "Let's practice opening a juice box," or "Next time, you could ask for help." You might suggest ideas by saying, "What do you think about having a set time and place to study?" or "It helps me to tell myself if I study for an hour, I can reward myself by doing something fun for an hour." Rather than telling them one "right" answer, make suggestions. Give them one or two acceptable solutions, and let them pick for themselves. This teaches them to make their own decisions, reminds them that you trust them, and stops them from thinking you're trying to run their lives.

"Give a man a fish, you feed him for a day; teach a man to fish,
you feed him for a lifetime."

—Anonymous

Vic used to say that he didn't expect his children to do many chores because it was easier for him to do them himself. That way, the chores would be done "properly." At fourteen, his son did not know how to make a bed, cook a meal, or use the washing machine. His son not only lacked skills, he also lacked confidence. By doing too much for his son, rather than allowing his son to struggle and fail, Vic did not set him up for success as an adult.

Sometimes, over-indulging a child is much easier to do than watching them struggle—much easier than watching them make mistakes. Setting them up so they can never make a mistake teaches them that you lack confidence in their ability to learn. It teaches them to be overly dependent on others. They grow up not only lacking skills, but also without a sense of how to learn new things.

At fifteen, Wes' daughter got a job with three-hour shifts. The job was twenty minutes away. Instead of indulging his daughter by giving her a bigger allowance, he allowed her an opportunity to learn responsibility by getting a job, even though it was inconvenient to Wes. It would have been cheaper and easier for him to give her money than drive forty minutes, wait an hour and a half, and do it again, Wes believed that to have his daughter learn responsibility and commitment was worth the inconvenience.

If the consequence of the mistake your child might make is too dangerous or damaging, it is more important to keep them safe. However, if it is an age-appropriate mistake, they will learn more if you let them experience the consequences for themselves. You can also discuss your own (and others') mistakes with your child. Children don't always understand that adults struggle. They think money "grows on trees" rather than realizing how hard we work for it. They think food magically appears on the table because they don't really know the process and planning it takes to feed a family. They think things are tough for them, but that things come easily to adults. They don't see our inner processes. They think we "just don't understand." If we share some of the mistakes we have made, then they will believe us when we tell them mistakes are normal and even helpful. We can tell them about the lessons we learned from budgeting mistakes that led us to becoming financially stable today. We can tell them the mistakes we made cooking that taught us how to put tasty food on the table. We can tell them the mistakes we made managing our anger that have taught us to control our temper now. We can show them that mistakes are expected and accepted, and that they are opportunities to learn and grow.

"Don't worry that children never listen to you; worry that they are always watching you."
—Robert Fulghum

List some mistakes you made as a child that taught you a lesson:

_____

_____

_____

How can you use these as examples to help your children learn?

_____

_____

_____

_____

How might you share this with your child?

_____

_____

_____

"Failure is the key to success; each mistake teaches us something."
—Morihei Ueshiba

Sharing your own mistakes, and allowing your children to make mistakes, also creates an environment in which they are not afraid to fail. We still wouldn't have light bulbs if Edison hadn't been afraid to fail...999 times! If we worry about making mistakes, we are more likely to make them. The phenomenon of "choking" in sports demonstrates this idea. If a basketball player is shooting free-throws for fun, they will succeed almost all the time. Put them on a court in front of thousands of fans when the score is close, and the fear of making a mistake increases the chance that they will miss. Basketball players miss more free-throws when the stakes are high than they do when they believe it's okay to make mistakes. Every tennis player can get their serve in the service box. Put them in front of thousands of fans at break point, and they are more likely to double fault. They convince themselves that double faulting—making a mistake—is unacceptable. Being afraid to make mistakes implies that mistakes are failures rather than learning opportunities. Knowing that mistakes are okay, expected, and even welcomed actually increases the likelihood of success.

Kehlani enjoyed musical theater, but she was always too afraid to try out for a part. Finally, she did try out for a play, and she got a part in the chorus. At the first rehearsal, the director gave the cast permission to "Make as many mistakes as it takes to become awesome." The director also explained that she would rather address mistakes in rehearsal than hear them for the first time on opening night. After the cast was given permission to make mistakes, tension decreased and so did the mistakes. On top of that, they had fun! As the actors learned their parts, some of them struggled with their lines, their dance moves, or their acting abilities. Because they knew mistakes were accepted, they became more creative. Some of their creative ideas were incorporated into the performance; some were not. But they would have never come up with new ideas if they hadn't been given permission to fail. The cast did a better job because they didn't worry about mistakes. Kehlani went on to try out for, and get parts in, many more plays.

Believing mistakes are not okay increases stress and makes mistakes more likely to happen. Believing mistakes are not okay increases defensiveness and justifications of bad behavior. Believing mistakes are normal, natural, and helpful creates an environment of safety, comfort, and optimal learning and growth.

"The most certain way to succeed is always to try just one more time."
—Thomas Edison

2

Listening to Feelings

A magic wand in the candy aisle

"The first duty of love is to listen."

—Paul Tillich

Children will listen to you better if you listen to them. If you talk more than you listen, your child will tune you out.

"Bore, n.: A person who talks when you wish him to listen."

—Ambrose Bierce

In 1980, Adele Faber and Elaine Mazlish wrote the timeless book *How to Talk So Kids Will Listen and Listen So Kids Will Talk*. While it covered much more than listening skills, its basic premise was that acknowledging your child's feelings is essential to good parenting. Faber and Mazlish wrote that many problems in parenting can be prevented by the simple practice of listening well. They also believed anything you do as a parent will be easier and more effective if you listen first.

Most of us have experienced wanting to talk about an important, upsetting, or critical event, only to have others jump in with unsolicited advice, judgment, or "one-up-manship." When we go to the doctor, we expect the doctor to listen to our list of symptoms before determining our illness and course of action; why would we not do the same with our children? When you listen to your children, they are more likely to consider any advice or adhere to any consequence. If you encourage your kids to talk, and allow yourself to listen, it may not take much more than a word or short phrase to get your point across. And, sometimes, the simple act of listening leads them to discovering that same point on their own.

"The greatest sign of success for a teacher...is to be able to say,
'The children are now working as if I did not exist.'"

—Maria Montessori

People generally enjoy talking about themselves. Kids do, too. They appreciate it when someone shows interest in their lives. Let your children talk. Listen to them. Maybe you'll find out more information that may change your response. Maybe they'll come to the same conclusion you were preparing to lecture them about. Without listening first, you may not give your child the specific help and guidance they are asking for.

Some listening methods draw people out, and some shut them down. To draw someone out, the first thing we can do is give them our full attention. When we give someone our full attention, they feel valued. When you are having an important phone conversation and your kids want attention, and you keep "shushing" them, do they keep quiet? If they are typical children, they tend to get louder. If you take a second or two to look them straight in the eyes, hold their hand even, and say, "Hey, as soon as I'm done talking, I promise you can show me your drawing," or "I really want to hear what you want to say, so if you wait a minute or two, I'll be able to listen to you without being distracted," or "We've talked about taking turns. It's Grandma's turn on the telephone. Soon I'll say goodbye to Grandma, and it will be your turn, and I won't let Grandma interrupt us," they may not leave you alone for the entire phone call, but it will work better than half-heartedly "shushing" them, and it certainly works better than yelling at them. Listening doesn't always work immediately, or perfectly, but it works better than discounting or ignoring.

Nancy was a professional who sometimes worked at home after the birth of her daughter. As most parents do, Nancy "multitasked." She put the dishes away while she was on the phone. She folded laundry as she watched TV. And she answered emails while she nursed her baby. She noticed very early on that if an email "dinged" while she was nursing, her baby began to squirm and fuss. If she looked at her baby, talked to her, or sang to her as she was nursing, her daughter didn't fuss, and the nursing session actually took less time. If Nancy thoughtfully and fully answered her emails with her full attention, fewer clarifying emails were needed. Giving her child her full attention, then giving her work her full attention saved time, and it was more pleasant than multi-tasking.

Giving your full attention saves time, prevents miscommunications, and promotes connection.

"No man ever listened himself out of a job."

—**Calvin Coolidge**

Sometimes life is busy, or we are not at our best. If we can't give our full attention, we can say, "I'm not able to give this my full attention right now; can we talk later?" or "My headache is so bad that it makes it hard to give you the attention you deserve; is it okay if I shut my eyes while we talk?" Some kids do better if you look them in the eyes, but for some kids, that's too much pressure. If face-to-face conversations feel too intimidating to your child, talking to them while making dinner, doing chores, or driving can work well. If doing something else as you talk with your child takes some pressure off them, that's wonderful. But multitasking to the point where your child does not feel like they have your full attention is likely to backfire. It is also important to make sure your child is able to give their full attention. Right before mealtime, they might be hungry and unable to give their full attention. If their emotions are too high to talk, give them your full attention with a hug until they are able to talk.

Once we give our full attention, what do we do? We can take a hint about listening to children from how we listen to our friends. If a friend is complaining about work, we tend to make those little noises, "hmm," "aw," "huh," and let them continue. Or we say those little phrases, "No way!" "They didn't?" "My goodness." This is the easiest way to let someone know we are listening and want to keep on listening. It's a simple skill. It's the same with kids. If we give them our full attention and use those words that encourage communication, they are more likely to talk to us.

"So when you are listening to somebody, completely, attentively, then you are listening not only to the words, but also to the feeling of what is being conveyed, to the whole of it, not part of it."
—Krishnamurti

Another easy way to get kids to keep talking is to restate the general idea of what they just said. If they complain that they have a lot of homework, you can say, "You're tired but still have tons of homework." If they complain that they don't want to eat their vegetables, you can say, "We always put vegetables on your plate that you don't want to eat." If they complain that their little brother went into their room without asking, you can say, "They didn't even knock—just went right in." This shows kids you are listening. Repeating what they say verbatim might just annoy them, so pick the main points, and put what they said into your own words. This is an easy way to keep someone talking.

> Mateo and his pre-teen daughter Camella had a strong father-daughter bond. One day, they were making breakfast together when out of the blue, Camella asked, "Where do babies come from?" *Oh, boy,* thought Mateo, *this is 'the talk.'* So, Mateo started explaining the "birds and the bees" to his daughter. She just looked at him with more and more confusion and awkwardness. Finally, he stopped to ask why she wanted to know where babies come from. "Well," she said, "chickens come from eggs, so how do I know that when I crack an egg for breakfast, a baby chick won't fall out?" Camella wasn't asking about the birds and the bees; she was asking about breakfast. If Mateo had simply said, "Hmm," or "Interesting question," or "You're wondering where babies come from?" Camella might have kept talking, and he would have known what she was actually asking about. If Mateo had encouraged her to talk a bit more, and listened a bit longer, the conversation would have been much different. Camella would have been much less confused.

Besides giving our friends cues to keep talking, we usually acknowledge and reflect their feelings. When a friend tells us about an unfair boss, we say, "So frustrating" or "That'd make anyone angry." When a friend tells us about a concert they want to see but can't afford tickets to, we say, "How disappointing" or "Bummer." Yet we often forget to do this with our children. We overlook the strong feelings they are relaying and jump ahead to solutions or advice. A friend complaining about a boss isn't looking for career advice, and a friend who can't afford concert tickets isn't looking for budgeting advice. (Even if they are, they probably aren't ready to hear that advice yet.) When children express strong feelings about a problem, they may already know the solution, but just like adults they want to complain a little first. If a child is told to do chores, but says, "I don't want to," they still know they have to do the chores. Yet parents jump in with, "Well, you have to." If instead, you said, "It's so hard to get motivated to do boring things," or "Chores suck," they would feel heard. Just that acknowledgment may be enough for your child to shamble off to do their chores. If not, then try advice and solutions. Your child is more likely to listen to advice and guidance, and even understand consequences, after you first listen to their feelings.

Reflecting their feelings not only teaches kids to identify feelings, but it lets them know you understand. Just saying, "I understand," is usually not enough. Your child may not believe you. Being more specific will show your child that you really do understand. If your child is angry about getting a bad grade, instead of saying, "I understand," you can show you understand by reflecting what happened and the feeling. "It is so frustrating when you study hard but still don't get a good grade. It can be disheartening" or "Expecting an A and getting a C can be a downer." Instead of telling your child, "You are angry" (which often leads to, "No, I'm not!" or "You don't know how I feel!"), you can say, "Experiencing such and such could make a person angry." That gives your child the ability to agree ("I *am* angry!") or disagree ("I'm not angry; I'm disappointed," or "I'm not angry; I'm furious!"). People rarely feel understood if you say, "I understand." If you show you understand by using reflective listening, you are demonstrating that you understand. If you don't have it quite right, your child can clarify what happened or what they feel.

"How we treasure (and admire) the people who acknowledge us!"
—Julie Morgenstern

After all, the feelings children have are the same feelings we all have. Adults don't like doing chores, get frustrated when we don't get something we want, and feel angry when we think something is unfair—just like children do.

When Emma took her kids to the store, like most children, they always asked for candy, cookies, and toys. "Can I have that?" "Why not?" "Why can't we buy that?" Shopping became one long "no" for Emma. "No, we can't." "No, we don't have the money for that." "No, you have enough toys." Emma was stressed, and her kids were disappointed. She tried telling them they could each pick out one treat, but they still asked, pleaded, and whined for more. One day when Emma was shopping alone at a clothing store, she realized she wanted all of the clothes she tried on, even though she could afford (and needed) only a few. She realized that was how her children felt at the grocery store. Everybody wants things they know they can't have. The next time Emma went shopping with her kids, she gave them each a magic wand (and made one for herself, too). She told her kids that they still would only get one treat, but each of them got to wave their magic wand at all the things they wanted but knew they couldn't buy. Emma showed empathy by also waving her magic wand at all the things she wanted and couldn't buy. By waving her magic wand at the ice cream, the expensive coffee drinks, and the pre-made meals, and then not buying them, her kids knew their mom understood. When Emma wanted something she couldn't have, she would say, "I really want that coffee, but I know I need to stay within my budget" or "I really want that prepared meal, but I know I can make it for half the cost. She taught her kids that it was normal to want things, but that even if you didn't get them, you could still be happy and content. Because they knew their mom understood, it was easier for them to accept reasonable boundaries. Shopping became a fun adventure instead of an exhausting argument.

Faber and Mazlish call this, "giving the child in fantasy what they can't have in reality." If you use this method of acknowledging a child's feelings, make sure it is a fantasy. If Emma had said to her kids, "Pick out all the things you want, but I'll only buy you one," they might still have expected her to buy the things they picked out. The magic wand let the kids know their mom understood their feelings, but that didn't mean she was buying them everything they wanted. You can say to a child who is complaining about homework, "Wouldn't it be nice if a Martian dropped out of the sky just to do your homework?" But don't say, "Wouldn't it be nice if you only had to do half a page of your homework?" You can say to a child who is complaining about chores, "Wouldn't it be nice if someone invented a self-cleaning house?" But don't say, "Wouldn't it be nice if your brother did all your chores?"

These methods—giving your children your full attention, using encouraging words, reflecting the situation, and acknowledging the underlying feelings—are all ways to show your kids you understand. Feeling heard and understood will encourage your kids to talk.

> *"Listening, not imitation, may be the sincerest form of flattery."*
> **—Dr. Joyce Brothers**

By using the examples of encouraging words, reflection of events, acknowledgment of feelings, or giving a fantasy solution, think of some different ways to respond to the following situations.

Your nine-year-old doesn't want to do their homework; instead of, "Everybody has to do their homework," you could say:

_____

_____

_____

_____

Your six-year-old doesn't want to eat what you prepared for dinner; instead of "There are starving children who would appreciate this food," you could say:

_____

_____

_____

_____

Your fifteen-year-old is angry about their curfew; instead of "My house, my rules," you could say:

_____

_____

_____

_____

Here are some examples:

Your nine-year-old doesn't want to do their homework; instead of, "Everybody has to do their homework," you could say, "It can feel like homework never ends." "Frustrating, huh?" "Wouldn't it be cool if you could invent a robot to do your homework for you?"

Your six-year-old doesn't want to eat what you prepared for dinner; instead of "There are starving children who would appreciate this food," you could say, "New food looks weird." "I bet when you saw that cauliflower, you thought, *What the heck is that?*" "Most people are scared to try new things, even new food."

Your fifteen-year-old is angry about their curfew; instead of "My house, my rules," you could say, "It's really hard having rules made for you that you don't agree with." "It's less fun to stay out with your friends if you have to worry about what time to be home." "Most people get mad when they think something is unfair."

> *"Humans aren't as good as we should be in our capacity to empathize with feelings and thoughts of others."*
>
> **—Neil deGrasse Tyson**

Listening is important. Sometimes just listening to your child solves the problem. Sometimes, you have to do more. While listening by itself won't solve every problem, it will help your child be more open to your suggestions. It will also clarify what the problem actually is. And it will make your child more willing to accept any lesson or consequence that comes next. With practice, these methods become easy. Most of us, however, have learned other methods for dealing with children who express strong negative feelings.

Here are some things to avoid:

Questioning:

It may seem that asking questions would encourage someone to share more, but questions can feel like badgering. Questions can make the other person feel like they have to defend themselves. Questions can also lead you away from what your child is trying to say. A statement like, "I want to hear more," works better than, "Why did you do that?"

Advice:

There is nothing wrong with advice. However, given too quickly, before listening to feelings, even amazing advice will probably be ignored. If you fully and completely listen, often a child will talk themselves into a solution. If they are stuck, you can say you have some ideas. They are more likely to listen to your advice after you listen to and acknowledge their feelings.

Minimizing or Pity:

Saying, "It wasn't so bad," "Aren't you overreacting?" or "Calm down," rarely makes someone want to share more. (Have you ever known anyone to actually calm down when someone tells them to?) Acknowledging feelings, even if we don't at first understand them, will bring out more information. If we say, "I can see how angry that makes you," it doesn't mean we are agreeing that it *should* make the other person angry; we are merely acknowledging that they are angry. We minimize feelings when we second-guess the reason our child is feeling their feelings. "You're just tired," or "It's just puppy love," usually produces defensiveness and arguments.

Platitudes and clichés are another way to minimize that rarely work. "It is what it is," "What did you expect?" and "Well, life isn't fair," don't help people feel heard. Even though the saying might be true, hearing it feels dismissive.

Pity, too, can be minimizing and make a person shut down. Unlike empathy, with pity, people feel "talked down to." Pity lets them know you don't think they are capable enough to handle their problems. And it can make them feel like you don't really want to hear what they have to say.

"Really listening and suspending one's own judgment is necessary in order to understand other people on their own terms.... This is a process that requires trust and builds trust."
—Mary Field Belenky

Paying attention to what your child is saying and feeling will help you understand what they need. Be quieter, give your full attention and allow your child to process on their own. You can empathize and still set firm limits on misbehavior. You can relate to the feelings your child is having and show them a way to manage them. You can even do this with a sense of fun. Encourage your child to talk by showing attention, reflection, curiosity, empathy, affection, and delight.

3

Importance of Feelings

Jumping in the deep end

"Our feelings are our most genuine paths to knowledge."

—Audre Lorde

Why is listening to feelings important? Can't we just jump to fixing the problem? Our feelings help us recognize what we value—they let us know what is important to us. Feelings reinforce the lessons we learn. Each feeling also brings with it unique and strategic gifts.

If I could wave a magic wand and you would never feel pain again, would you want me to do it? The quick answer is, "Yes, of course!" Why would anyone want to feel pain? But think about it for a minute. What would happen the next time you touched a hot stove? You wouldn't immediately know to move your hand away. You might not notice until your hand was badly burned. After you've moved your hand and learned not to touch a hot stove, you don't need to feel that pain anymore. The pain has served its purpose. If you didn't feel the pain of a cavity, you might not know to seek treatment until your tooth was too damaged to save. After you call the dentist, you don't need to feel that pain anymore because you've already recognized what you needed to do, and done it. What would happen if you had appendicitis and didn't feel pain? You could die. How would you know when you've pushed your body too far while working, playing, or exercising? Pain, while unpleasant, has a purpose. It exists to protect us from further injury.

What if I waved a magic wand, and you never felt fear again? You didn't feel fear at any level, no nervousness, no anxiety, no worry. Would you want that? At first, again, you might say, "Yes," but how would you determine whether something was safe? Why wouldn't you jump off a bridge into a river without knowing how deep the water was? How fast would you drive? Why would you study for a test if you weren't a little bit afraid you might fail? Fear is a warning signal.

While we may want to protect our children from feeling sad, doing so can disconnect them from others.

Sadness reminds us of connection. Sadness connects us to people and important events. Would you worry about someone who didn't feel sad when a loved one died? That might indicate that they weren't connected to the deceased or to their own emotions. Would you worry about your child if they didn't feel sad when they heard a story about a sad, lonely puppy? The ability to feel sadness is the ability to feel empathy and relationship to others.

"There is a sacredness in tears. They are not the mark of weakness, but of power. They speak more eloquently than ten thousand tongues. They are the messengers of overwhelming grief, of deep contrition, and of unspeakable love."

—Washington Irving

If I waved my magic wand so you would never feel angry again, would you want me to wave it? Again, at first, you might say yes; however, anger is what we feel when we think something is unfair or unjust. To fight unfairness and/or injustice, we need courage, focus, and determination. These are gifts that anger gives us.

When we think of Gandhi, we think of calmness and non-violence. But Gandhi got mad. When he was a young man, he took a train through India to South Africa. Coming from a wealthy family, he had paid for a first-class ticket. Part way through his journey, he was asked to move to third class because of the color of his skin. He thought it was unjust. After all, he had paid for a first-class ticket. He argued with a rail worker and was forcibly removed from the train. In his autobiography, Gandhi says that he was so angry that he sat for hours, thinking about racism, inequality, and injustice. As he sat and thought, he developed his idea of passive resistance. Even though he felt angry, he did not let his anger push him to violence. He chose to sit and think. He used his anger to fuel his mind rather than cloud it. Some would argue that he felt determination or resolve, not anger. However, his anger at being treated unjustly led to his resolve.

"Anger is a signal and one worth listening to."

—Harriet Lerner

It is important to separate the feeling of anger from the behavior of violence. Anger can make us so brave, focused, and determined that we forget about other considerations and lash out violently, but it doesn't have to.

Anger lets us know what is important to us, it helps us recognize injustice, it protects us, and it gives us the energy and single-mindedness we need to take action.

These are important gifts from anger. You want to hold on to these gifts. You want to eliminate behavior that gets you in trouble, but you don't want to eliminate anger. Anger tends to linger under the surface if you ignore it. Often, when people try to banish their anger, it comes out at other times or in other ways. Have you ever been really, really angry about something but not shown it, and then something really little and unimportant happens and you blow up? Have you ever seen other people do this? Have you seen your children do this? There are ways to acknowledge anger and take action without causing trouble or hurting others. If anger is not acknowledged in *some* way, it very well may come out later.

"When you own or take responsibility for your feelings, you place yourself in a position of power and control."

—Julie A. Ross and Judy Corcoran

We can ask these questions about all the emotions we typically think of as "negative" emotions. Guilt reminds us of our values and helps us stay on our moral path. Jealousy might push us to achieve more.

Emotions may influence our behavior, but they don't force us to do anything. Pain lets us know injury might occur, but we decide what we are going to do about it. Fear lets us know there might be danger; then we decide what to do. Anger is a warning sign that something may be unjust; then it is our decision what steps we take. Sadness lets us know something matters to us that we don't want to lose.

Following your emotions without thinking can get you in just as much trouble as ignoring them. What if you decided that since a vaccine shot hurt, it should be avoided? Or what if we thought the pain of a dentist visit was to be avoided? What if we felt fear about doing something we really want to do, like trying out for the school play? Fear, pain, sadness, and anger can keep us from our goals if we follow them blindly, without thinking about those feelings and what is causing them.

We may be scared to speak in public but do so anyway. We may be scared to skydive and choose not to. We may feel sadness when we hear a friend has suffered a loss and decide to call them up or visit them. We may feel sadness watching a sad movie, but then we move on. Injustice may bring up anger that pushes us to take action for social change. A bad call by the coach of our favorite football team may make us angry, but we choose to do nothing about it.

Name some times when you hurt, but chose to *push through the pain*:

_____

_____

_____

_____

Name some times you were hurt and knew it was time to quit:

_____

_____

_____

_____

Name some things you are afraid of that you choose to do anyway:

_____

_____

_____

_____

Name some things you are afraid of and choose not to do:

_____

_____

Give some examples of when your anger fueled helpful behavior:

_____

_____

_____

_____

Give some examples of when your anger fueled harmful behavior:

_____

_____

_____

_____

Anger often masks pain, fear, and sadness. When some people feel hurt, they express it as anger. Sometimes, underneath anger there is actually fear. And sometimes, if we experience loss, we respond with anger because the sadness hurts too much. If your child is acting angry, underneath, they may actually be feeling scared, sad, or hurt.

Think of some times when anger might mask pain:

_____

_____

_____

_____

Think of some times when anger might mask fear:

_____

_____

_____

_____

Think of some times when anger might mask sadness:

_____

_____

_____

_____

If someone is uncomfortable expressing anger, their anger might get transformed into pain, fear, or sadness. If you are uncomfortable with anger, you may find yourself feeling sad, scared, or hurt. If your child is uncomfortable with anger, their anger may show itself as sadness, fear, or pain.

Think of some times when anger might show itself as sadness:

_____

_____

_____

_____

Think of some times when anger might show itself as fear:

_____

_____

_____

_____

Think of some times when anger might show itself as pain:

_____

_____

_____

_____

All feelings can help us recognize our values. We feel pain, fear, sadness, anger, and other strong emotions about things important to us. Feelings tell us what to focus on. Feelings bring our attention to what is going on around us and help us make decisions. Feelings also help us follow through on the decisions we make. Additionally, they each have their particular gifts to help us follow through with our decisions. Pain informs us we might injure ourselves. Fear makes us more cautious and careful. Anger creates bravery and focus. Sadness brings empathy and helps us connect to those we love. Feelings point us in the right direction. Feelings also help us stay on a difficult path.

"Feelings are really your GPS system for life. When you're supposed
to do something, or not supposed to do something,
your emotional guidance system lets you know."

—Oprah Winfrey

Feelings are as important as thinking. Help your children recognize, monitor, and manage their feelings. Talk to your children about the benefits and drawbacks of their sadness, anger, fear, guilt, boredom, and every other emotion. Share with them your own methods of managing feelings. Teach them your moral principles about when, whether, and how to express feelings. Help your child see the messages their feelings bring them. Help them realize they can decide what to do about the messages their feelings bring.

"Maybe part of our formal education should be training in empathy.
Imagine how different the world would be if, in fact,
that were 'reading, writing, arithmetic, empathy.'"

—Neil deGrasse Tyson

Adults can find their emotions difficult to control. How many of us have let our anger control our behavior? Imagine how much more difficult emotional control is for a child—especially for a child who hasn't been given any guidance or tools and hasn't been allowed to practice. When we teach our children emotional management, they will make mistakes. Each mistake they make while trying to choose positive behaviors when feeling strong emotions is a teaching opportunity.

Benjamin commonly did what most of us do when our child is angry. When his five-year-old son, Spencer, got angry, he yelled, "Go to your room, and don't come out until you calm down!" And then he thought about how he would respond to other emotions. He wouldn't say the same thing to his son if he expressed sadness or fear. He wouldn't say to a crying child, "Go to your room, and don't come out until you are happy again." He wouldn't say to a frightened child, "Go to your room until you are confident and strong."

We expect our children to know how to manage their emotions, even though we have not given them the tools and opportunities to do so. If we don't teach our children to manage their emotions, how can we expect them to know how? We teach our kids to brush their teeth, clean their rooms, and drive a car. We don't expect them to know automatically how to do those things. But, for some reason, we expect our kids to know, without being taught, how to manage their emotions.

"So often, children are punished for being human. They are not allowed to have grumpy moods,
bad days, disrespectful tones, or bad attitudes. Yet, we adults have them all the time. None of us
are perfect. We must stop holding our children to a higher standard of perfection than we can
attain ourselves."

—Rebecca Eanes

Anger, in particular, is an emotion we expect children to overcome without any training. It is also an emotion we restrict more than most.

"Anybody can become angry—that is easy, but to be angry with the right person and to the right degree and at the right time and for the right purpose and in the right way—that is not within everybody's power and is not easy."

—Aristotle

Besides giving our kids room to understand their anger, we also need to model anger management for them. Kids don't see the internal process of adults managing emotions. They don't see us count to ten in our heads when we are frustrated. They don't realize that when we leave the room to cook dinner, we are giving ourselves a time-out. They don't hear the practiced self-talk we use to calm ourselves. They think we automatically know how to calm down.

One way to teach our children how to manage their anger is to model how we manage our own anger. We can do this by slowing down our process so that they can witness it. We can say, "I'm getting angry. I need to walk into the kitchen to take a time-out." Or "I'm frustrated right now, so I'm going to think about lying on a warm beach until I feel calmer." Or "I'm starting to feel like I might lose control, so I'm going to take a deep breath and count to ten." We probably employ these things automatically, without thinking about them. It may take us some time to recognize the skills we, ourselves, use to calm down. Once we do become aware of the skills we use, we can model them for our children.

Every household has its own rules. What is necessary is that kids have *some* way of expressing their anger that helps them calm down and doesn't get them in trouble. Time-outs, if they are presented as a way to limit stimuli rather than as a punishment, may be one way. Taking deep breaths, going for a walk, drawing an angry picture, breaking crayons—these are ways people calm down. Not every action works for every person. Breaking crayons is only a good suggestion if it is acceptable in your family, and if it actually calms your child down. If your child gets angrier breaking crayons, or if they regret breaking something they like, it's not a helpful anger management technique.

Julie struggled with finding a way to help her twelve-year-old son, Arty, safely and helpfully express his anger. None of the typical suggestions, like using his words, time-outs, counting to ten, talking, writing, or punching a pillow, seemed to work. Arty needed something very active and wanted something that made him feel powerful when he was angry. He didn't yet have the ability to choose a productive activity that also calmed his anger. Julie didn't want to teach Arty that destroying something was an acceptable way to express anger, but nothing else seemed to work. So, Julie sat down with Arty and discussed strategies to express anger that worked for Arty, but were also acceptable to Julie. They decided to save all the boxes that needed to be smashed flat to be put in the recycling bin. When Arty was angry, he could go on the back porch and stomp on the recycling. After Arty learned to express his anger by smashing boxes, he could then expand his anger management strategies to include things that didn't necessarily involve destroying something.

For some kids, drawing works well; for others, it doesn't help at all. In some families, it is okay to punch a pillow; in other families, it isn't. Some kids seem to need something very active to express their anger. Some kids need something creative. Some kids need to talk to others. Some kids do better alone. If taking a deep breath doesn't seem to work for your child, maybe drawing an angry picture will. There are as many ways to calm down as there are children.

Anger is a feeling. It easily leads to certain behaviors, such as arguments and violence, but it doesn't have to. No matter how angry we are, our behavior is still our choice. There are many examples throughout history of people who felt angry but used that anger in a non-violent way to promote change. People were angry that women didn't have the right to vote, so they marched. People were angry at segregation, so they boycotted. People were angry about deaths caused by drunk drivers, so they formed a grass-roots movement, Mothers Against Drunk Driving (MADD), and changed laws. We can harness our anger, like we harness fire, for good. Fire, out of control, is dangerous; fire, contained and controlled, is very helpful. It is the same with anger. Out of control, it can lead to violence; contained and controlled, it can be a powerful force for positive change.

In 1874, neighbors became angry when they saw a mother repeatedly beating her adopted daughter with whips. The neighbors appealed to the law, but found there were no laws against beating your child. A reporter, Etta Angell Wheeler, investigated the situation and became so angry about the abuse and the lack of laws protecting children that she decided to change the law. With the help of a lawyer, she took the case to the New York State Supreme Court, charging that mother with "cruelty to animals" since there were laws against whipping your horse, but none against whipping your child. The state supreme court listened, and Etta Wheeler's outrage and anger pushed her to champion the first laws against child abuse.

Because children can't see the internal struggle adults go through when managing their emotions, we need to let them know managing emotions is a skill they can learn and master. We need to make it clear we don't expect them to have that skill before they are taught it. We say, "Go to your room until you're not angry anymore." That's like saying to a three-year-old, "Go to your room, and don't come out until you're potty trained," or telling a nine-year-old, "Go to your room until you understand multiplication, and don't come out until you're done!"

> Mia loved to sing as a child, but she didn't think she was talented or had a good voice. Then a friend gave her a gift certificate for voice lessons. At her first lesson, she told her teacher she wasn't a good singer. Her teacher told her something she hadn't thought of before. "Some people are naturally talented, with perfect pitch and a good voice. Singing comes naturally to them. But most people have to be taught. Singing is no different than any other skill. Someone has to teach us to read, to bake a cake, to use a skill saw. Why would singing be any different?" With this new understanding, Mia found she could enjoy learning how to sing and she even ended up joining a choir after a few months of lessons.

Fear teaches us caution and to be prepared.

List some helpful things you say or do when you are scared:

_____

_____

_____

_____

List some helpful things your child can say or do when they are scared:

_____

_____

_____

_____

Anger gives us drive and determination.

List some helpful things you do or say to calm yourself when you are angry:

_____

_____

_____

_____

List some helpful things your kids can do or say to calm themselves when they are angry:

_____

_____

_____

_____

Sadness reminds us of what is important and keeps us connected to the things that matter to us.

List some helpful things you do or say when you are sad:

_____

_____

_____

_____

List some helpful things your child can do or say to let you know they are sad:

_____

_____

_____

_____

Teaching children to manage their emotions starts with listening to and acknowledging their feelings. Then, it's about reminding them that their emotions are normal. Everyone gets mad, feels afraid, and is sad at times. We can share with our children the helpful methods we use to manage our own emotions. If we are having trouble managing our own emotions, we can learn and practice this process with our children. We all need to have some way to safely and constructively express emotions. Expressions will be different for different families, but there has to be some acceptable way to express emotions. It should be safe, it should work, and it shouldn't get anyone in trouble.

Teresa was a single mom with a ten-year-old son, Trevor. Trevor's teacher said he had an "anger management problem." Teresa had left an abusive relationship, so Trevor had seen his dad hit and kick his mom. After hitting his mom, Trevor's dad would say he did it because she "made him mad." Trevor sometimes felt mad at his mom, like most kids do. He also loved and cared for his mom and didn't want to hurt her. But sometimes she "made him mad." Teresa talked to Trevor about anger. She talked to him about the positive aspects of anger. She also talked to him about what behavior was okay and what behavior was not okay, no matter how angry he got. Trevor was struggling with how to feel anger without hurting anyone. They problem-solved ways that were safe, that worked, and that wouldn't get anyone in trouble. Teresa talked to the teacher and asked if Trevor could keep play-dough in his desk at school so when he felt angry, he could knead the play-dough.

It's helpful to think of emotions as ranging from low to high, like a volume control. We don't have to turn our emotions all the way off, but sometimes it's helpful to turn the intensity of them up or down.

Lucas was afraid of the water when Liam took him to his first swimming lesson. The teacher suggested that Liam get in the water to show Lucas it was safe. Lucas began to feel safe in the water. To show how comfortable he felt, after his very first swimming lesson, Lucas jumped in the deep end of the pool. Liam realized he wanted Lucas's fear to be turned down a bit, but not turned all the way off.

Different things work in different households. Different things work for different people. If jumping on boxes makes your child less angry, great; if it makes your child angrier, help them find something else.

Managing feelings is a difficult skill to learn. Have patience with your children. Remember how difficult it is for you to manage your own feelings, especially when you are feeling unheard, alone, overwhelmed, or even merely tired.

4

Discipline

Let's Misbehave!

"A person who has been punished is not less inclined to behave in a given way; at best, he learns how to avoid punishment."

—B. F. Skinner

Punishments tends to be either too quick, like a spanking, or too lengthy, like grounding. A quick punishment doesn't give a child enough time to think about their behavior. A lengthy punishment gives the child too much time to think about how unfair their parents are.

"Punishment is what you do to someone; discipline is what you do for someone."

—Zig Ziglar

Punishment is only one meaning of discipline. Another definition is closer to self-discipline; calm and controlled behavior. A disciple is a follower, student of a teacher, or leader. To discipline means to lead and teach responsibility, skills, and values. Discipline without punishment is not more indulgent or lenient; it is more effective.

Effective parenting is similar to effective teaching. We learned from the good teachers we had, and we liked and respected them. If we had a teacher we liked and respected, we tried to live up to their expectations and we kept our behavior in check. We perform best not out of fear of punishment, but out of the desire to please them.

Think back on a teacher you liked and respected. Think of a teacher who not only helped you learn, but helped you be excited about learning, a teacher whom you felt liked and respected you. It can be a teacher you had in school or a mentor who helped you through a difficult time. When we think of favorite teachers, we remember wanting to please them, behaving for them, and also learning from them. We did so because we wanted to please our teachers, not because we feared punishment. We behave our best out of a desire to please those we respect and who respect us.

As a parent, you can model yourself after a good teacher. Besides respecting and liking them, you probably learned more in their classes. You may remember how to conjugate verbs in Spanish because, in class thirty years ago, your Spanish teacher had high expectations but also made learning fun. You may have hated math, but you worked hard in trigonometry because your teacher made it interesting and respected your struggle.

List the qualities of one of your favorite teachers:

_____

_____

_____

_____

How did this teacher make you feel?

_____

_____

_____

_____

What did you think about this teacher?

_____

_____

_____

_____

When we think of our favorite teachers, we rarely find attributes associated with punishment. We find qualities associated with respect. Respect incorporates both kindness and high expectations. These are the qualities that help us learn best. Punishment mostly teaches us how to avoid punishment. Thinking of discipline like a teacher is a different concept from thinking of discipline as punishment.

Some qualities people recall when describing their favorite teachers are: respectful, helpful, funny, kind, peaceful, patient, quiet, trusting, accepting, self-accepting, empathetic, generous, non-critical, unthreatening, flexible, challenging, realistic, tough, fair, skilled, clear, passionate, inclusive, brave, confident, competent, and responsible. They describe teachers who: listened, gave them time, explored options, planned, involved them, had consequences, had a relationship with them, saw them as individuals, looked past flaws, enjoyed challenges, inspired confidence, gave "boosts," and used humor.

When people describe how their favorite teachers made them feel, they say things like: safe, secure, loved, accepted, good, understood, capable, safe to explore and make mistakes, listened to, valued, hopeful, confident, competent, on track, brave, and grateful. Isn't that how we want our children to feel about us?

The thoughts they have about their favorite teachers are, "I want to be like them," "It's my choice," "It's my responsibility," "They are classy," "They are proud of me," "They'll protect me," "They'll defend me," "I love them," "They stand up for their ideals," "They are human and make mistakes," "They are emotionally safe," "They know me," "They know what I can and can't handle," "They are smart." Isn't this what we want our children to think about us?

Students put forth their best effort for these teachers. A good teacher not only has the qualities of respect and kindness, but a good teacher actually shows expertise in their subject area.

Kids do respond to punishment, but it also has several drawbacks. While their behavior may improve, they learn more about avoiding punishment than improving their behavior. When you were punished as a child, how much time did you spend reflecting on your behavior? How much time did you spend resenting your parents or thinking they were unfair? If you think back, I'll bet you remember instances of punishment more distinctly than you remember the behavior you were punished for. We remember the spankings, the time-outs, and the groundings, but we forget our own misbehavior.

Children who are punished learn that the reason to behave is to avoid punishment. They don't understand that behaving well has actual and natural benefits. It's good for kids to brush their teeth, to eat their vegetables, to do their homework. It's good for kids to have regular chores and regular bedtimes. It's good for kids to come home when they're supposed to. Parents don't make up these rules just to torment their children. Parents know these rules will actually benefit their children. But often, children think the rules are arbitrary and made merely to limit their freedom and fun. Sometimes kids do something and their parents punish them, when they do the same thing another time, and their parents let it go unpunished. Kids tend to think punishments are random, or that their parents are mean, rather than associating punishments with behavior that might be bad for them. Kids tend to believe that punishment is about their parents' emotions rather than about their parents teaching them. If you discipline instead of punish, if you teach instead of react, your children have a better chance of learning the reason behind the rules.

"I've learned that people will forget what you said, people will forget what you did, but people will never forget how you made them feel."

—Maya Angelou

There are certain things we think of when we think of punishment. Think of the ways your parents punished you or ways parents commonly punish their children. What kind of list would you come up with?

List ways your parents punished you or ways other parents punished their children:

_____

_____

_____

_____

The list you come up with may include spanking, slapping, pinching, yelling, grounding, shaming, "guilting," lecturing, giving time outs, restricting fun activities, removing games, restricting privileges, name-calling, threatening, banishing to corners, rooms, or beds, leaving, removing love, or giving up.

Now, think back to when you were punished as a child, and tell me how you felt: How did you feel about your behavior? How did you feel about the punishment? How did you feel about your parents?

List how these punishments made you feel:

_____

_____

_____

_____

This list usually includes things like: angry, pissed off, scared, fearful, sad, wronged, unheard, silenced, abandoned, resentful, confused, misunderstood, alone, shamed, bored, unloved, misunderstood, hurt, distanced, traumatized, hateful, guilty, relieved, and manipulated. It usually doesn't include feelings such as: repentant, thoughtful, grateful, aware, considerate, and thoughtful. As a child, you probably didn't believe the punishment was justified. Instead, you thought your parents were mean or they just didn't understand. When kids believe their punishment is unfair, instead of contemplating their own behavior, they think about ways to argue about how unfairly they have been treated. They come up with excuses for their behavior. They may even brood on ways to "get back" at their parents.

What were your thoughts about the punishments you received as a child?

_____

_____

_____

_____

You might have thought, "I wish they'd just shut up," "Blah, blah, blah," "They can ruin my life," "It's a game," "Why are they mad now?" "They don't understand," "If only I could explain," "It's unfair," "It's not my fault," "I have to be perfect," "I'm going to get you back," "I want them to suffer," "This is a battle, and I'm going to win," "*They* don't take responsibility, why should I?" "I hate you!" or "You're mean!"

One reason kids don't listen to us is that we fail to show them we have expertise at teaching good behavior. We don't take them through the process of how to change their behavior; we just expect them to change it. We don't give them examples of better ways to behave. We don't encourage questions. We don't find them opportunities to practice. We tell them, "That's wrong!" We tell them, "Be good!" We tell them, "Behave," but we don't teach them how to behave. We say to our children, "I hope you learned your lesson." But how can they learn a lesson if they were never taught?

List how you felt when you were corrected by your favorite teacher:

_____

_____

_____

You may have felt listened to, understood, respected, helped, curious, or self-reflecting. Because you respected your teacher, and knew they respected you, you probably didn't feel "picked on." You may have even believed that the correction was reasonable and maybe even helpful. If the reprimand was given without shaming you, without attacking you, without punishing you, you were more likely to correct your behavior willingly for that favorite teacher. As a "well-disciplined" student, you were not only willing, but pleased and proud to change your behavior.

How did you feel about this teacher, even when they were tough?

_____

_____

_____

_____

Many people say they felt respected, helped, contemplative, empathetic, heard, attentive, understood, introspective, and even appreciative. They felt safe with this teacher. They wanted to please this teacher. How you felt about a teacher when they set limits or called you out on your behavior is usually very similar to how you felt about that teacher in general.

Ron was having trouble disciplining his stepdaughter. He thought of "disciplining" as yelling, lecturing, and grounding. Ron was a recovering alcoholic and had a sponsor, someone who encouraged him, supported him, and helped him. Ron thought about the qualities his sponsor had that were most helpful, which were similar to those of a good teacher. Ron listed qualities like empathy, confidence, respect, knowledge, experience, kindness, understanding, and open-mindedness. He also listed qualities like strong, persistent, tough, fair, and honest. His sponsor was understanding and accepting, but also challenged Ron and set high standards. Then Ron thought about how he treated his stepdaughter. It was very different from how his sponsor treated him. Ron felt comfortable going to his sponsor with failures and mistakes. He felt supported. Most importantly, he learned from his sponsor and was able to continue healthy behaviors and avoid unhealthy ones. As Ron began to treat his stepdaughter more and more like his sponsor treated him, her behavior improved and their relationship also improved. His stepdaughter trusted him enough to come to him with concerns before they became problems.

When your children misbehave, call to mind your favorite teacher. It is unfortunate that our own emotions run high when our kids misbehave. We might be frustrated, worried, or angry. It can be difficult to think of ourselves as teachers when we are upset. It is easier to lash out. However, if you think of discipline as teaching rather than punishing, you can change your response from reactive to proactive. If you model yourself after a teacher you respected and admired, who was competent, but who was also tough and fair, your children are more likely to learn. Thinking of discipline as teaching can help your children learn how to change their behavior rather than merely learning how to avoid punishment.

5

Discipline Strategies

Can't you just spank me and get it over with?

"Don't handicap your children by making their lives easy."
—Robert A Heinlein

We do need to respond when our children do something they aren't supposed to do. It is important to stop negative behaviors, we can't ignore them. But there are alternatives to punishment that are much more effective. Yelling, grounding, spanking, and similar punishments work to some extent, but the drawbacks outweigh the benefits.

List some drawbacks of typical punishments:

_____

_____

_____

_____

When they are punished, kids might resort to hiding their behavior, lying, or adopting other unhelpful behaviors, especially if they don't understand the underlying reason behind the punishment. If your goal is to help your child think about their behavior and learn why to stop it, not just how to stop it, natural and logical consequences work best. Using consequences instead of punishment does not mean ignoring negative behavior—and it does not mean making things easy on your kids.

Punishment is very "black and white." Kids who are punished learn that behavior is either right or wrong instead of realizing that bad behavior has consequences. We want our kids to learn that the reason not to do undesirable behavior is that it brings undesirable results, whether anyone is there to punish them or not. One of the negative outcomes of punishment is that those who have been punished often have difficulty seeing different perspectives. When children are spanked, it may be harder for them to learn open-mindedness, tolerance, and consideration.

Sean's first response to hearing about consequences rather than punishment was, "My parents spanked me, and I turned out fine." Spankings taught him to stop doing the things that caused the spankings, but he never really learned why. His behavior was mechanical, with little thought behind it at all. He realized that perhaps his unwillingness to see alternatives to spanking might be a result of not learning to think about his behavior when he was a kid. He didn't want to coddle his kids, but he was finally convinced to try to discipline without spanking. He began to think of himself as a teacher and used logical consequences. He realized that consequences pushed his kids to think about their behavior rather than think about ways to hide their behavior from him. He knew he was on the right track when, after misbehaving, his daughter said, "Can't you just spank me and get it over with?"

Punishment doesn't work because punishment doesn't teach. Punishment denies kids the opportunity to really think about their behavior. If a kid is spanked after misbehaving, in their mind the situation is resolved. They don't need to think about it anymore. With natural or logical consequences, the kid continues to think about their behavior because they can see the direct link between their behavior and the consequence.

If our child isn't doing something they should be doing, we often jump to the conclusion that they just don't want to do it, so we lecture them about responsibility. However, there may be several reasons why they aren't doing as we want them to. One is simply that they don't have the information they need. Telling them that wet towels on the floor breed bacteria might be all it takes to get them to pick up their wet towels. Telling them that chunks of food left on the plate when you put it in the dishwasher get stuck in the filter and can cause a clog might be just what it takes to remind them to rinse their dishes. Telling them that slamming the door weakens the hinges or disturbs the neighbors might help them not to slam the door so often. One way to address some misbehavior is to simply give information.

Think of something you simply didn't know as a child that got you in trouble:

_____

_____

_____

_____

Your child may think they know what you are asking them to do when they don't fully understand what is being asked. It is common for parents to tell children to clean their rooms, and the child says, "I did!" Then the parent looks in the room and says, "No you didn't. Now, go in there and clean your room!" The problem may simply be that the parent and child have a different understanding of what a "clean room" is. Your child might need specific information: "A clean room means no clothes, toys, or books on the floor, the bed made, and the carpet vacuumed everywhere a person can walk."

Mary Ellen was frustrated that her son, Lee, always seemed to leave crumbs when it was his job to wipe down the counters. He would be playing a game, and she would walk into the kitchen and see crumbs on the counter. She would yell at him that he wasn't supposed to play until he finished his chores. He would yell back that he had finished his chores. Then she realized she hadn't been specific enough about his responsibilities. She was surprised at the improvement when she gave simple instructions about what it meant to clean the kitchen. She told Lee that bacteria grew on things that were damp, so part of wiping the counters was putting the dirty dish towels in the wash. She told Lee there were two reasons to wipe counters: to get sticky stuff off, and to wipe all the crumbs and food debris off the counters. She also explained that the reason for that was to prevent ants from invading the kitchen and to keep other dishes and food clean when preparing the next meal. Cinnamon toast would taste pretty bad if it were made on a countertop where someone had just made garlic toast and not wiped the counter. Lee was not being difficult; he was willing to wipe the counters; he just did not understand his mother's expectations. Clear information stopped Mary Ellen from thinking that Lee was lazy or defiant, and stopped Lee from thinking his mom was unrealistic and "naggy."

Even when kids have all the information, they may still be lacking the skill to do what you expect of them. Some kids are just too young to remember to turn in their homework. Some kids don't know how to self-soothe, so telling them to calm down just isn't going to help because they literally don't know how to calm themselves down. Ensure that your child has the skills to do the jobs you give them. If they don't, you can reevaluate and adjust if your expectations aren't age-appropriate, or you can help them learn the skills they need.

If we believe our child understands and has the skills needed to do what is expected, but still isn't doing what is expected, we can move to natural consequences or logical consequences. Natural and logical consequences allow children to reflect on their own behavior, learn to see others' points of view, and maintain positive relationships with their parents. When we allow natural or logical consequences, children are more apt to see a reason behind our rules and that their behavior led directly to the consequence. Then they understand the consequence isn't something imposed upon them; it is something they created by their behavior.

Natural consequences occur so naturally that, as parents, we can just sit back and be ready to provide explanation or even sympathy after the fact. The natural consequence to forgetting your jacket is that you are cold. The natural consequence of forgetting your lunch is that you are hungry. The natural consequence of leaving your clothes on the floor is that they don't get washed. The natural consequence of cutting a hole in a juice box is that the juice spills out all over the floor. Logical consequences are what we use when natural consequences aren't safe or appropriate.

Diane had trouble getting her seventh grader, Amber, to put her clothes in the hamper. Amber was at an age when appearance really mattered to her. Instead of yelling or nagging, and instead of putting the clothes in the hamper herself, Diane allowed the consequences to naturally occur. After a week and a half, Amber came to Diane and asked, "Where is my red top? I want to wear it today." "I'm not sure," said Diane. Amber looked at her mother with frustration. "I need to wear it today!" Amber began picking up and throwing all the clothes she had left on the floor around her room. "Here it is! Why didn't you wash it?" she accused Diane. Diane calmly said, "I wash what's in the hamper. I'm happy to show you how to use the washing machine if you want to take over the job of washing your clothes." Amber looked at Diane in astonishment. "It's not my job to wash my clothes! That's your job!" "Well," Diane said, " You don't like me to go into your room, and I don't like yelling at you or nagging you, so I'm going to make it easy on both of us," and she repeated that she would wash the clothes in the hamper. Or, if Amber preferred, she could show her how to use the washing machine. Amber was still frustrated and angry, but it was hard to blame her mom

What are the natural consequences if your child keeps forgetting to put the cap on the markers they are using?

_____

_____

_____

_____

What happens if your child doesn't study for a test?

_____

_____

_____

_____

What happen if your child refuses to put their clothes in the hamper?

_____

_____

_____

_____

Think of some examples of where you can replace yelling or nagging with natural consequences:

_____

_____

_____

_____

Kids might feel that natural consequences are still unfair or excessive, but natural consequences make it easier for them to see the connection between their behavior and the consequence, and make it harder for them to blame their parents. Natural consequences can also be initiated by the child themselves.

Keith wanted a computer game. Money was tight, so his mom, Julie, told him they couldn't afford it. "Fine!" shouted Keith. "I'll just do yard work for the neighbors and earn the money myself!"

Julie secretly celebrated that her son had found his own solution, was learning responsibility, and learning the value of money.

Rules have a purpose. Kids tend to think they are random—or even made up to make their lives miserable. "Why do I have to have a bedtime?" "I don't want to brush my teeth!" "I don't like broccoli!" Natural consequences clarify the reason behind our rules. We have a reason we want our kids to do well in school, come home on time, and not eat food in their bedrooms.

> Rick was thirteen, but it was still a struggle for his dad, Fred, to get him to brush his teeth. While Fred wasn't willing to let Rick suffer the long-term consequences of cavities, he was still able to find natural consequences that showed Rick why he needed to brush his teeth. Fred asked Rick to scrape his fingernail over the gum line of his teeth, then look at the gunk that he scraped off. Even a thirteen-year-old boy found that gross. Since Rick was just starting to be interested in girls, Fred also asked Rick to cup his hands over his mouth and smell his own breath. What girl would want to be close enough to slow dance with him with that breath?

The best way to use natural consequences is to tell your child once (or twice) what the natural consequences will be if they continue a behavior. If they continue the behavior, the natural consequences will happen. They will learn that the actual consequence of leaving the markers out is that they dry out; they will learn that they get better grades on a test if they study; they will learn that if they don't put their clothes in the hamper, they won't have clean clothes to wear; they will learn that no one wants to kiss someone with bad breath. If you tell them once or twice and then step back, your children will also learn how smart you are! If we repeat our warning too many times, our kids will think we are nagging. If we don't allow the natural consequences to occur (for example, if we angrily pick up our children's dirty clothes), they may never learn the natural consequences.

> When Hector's daughter, Carmen, was about eight years old, she came inside on a very hot day after playing with friends and was very thirsty. Hector watched as Carmen poured herself a tall glass of grape juice. He let her know that even though she felt very, very thirsty, it was probably not a good idea to drink so much grape juice so fast. She ignored him and drank the juice. Then she poured herself another full glass. She drank that, too. After about ten seconds, she threw up the two full glasses of grape juice all over the kitchen floor. They calmly cleaned it up together, and Hector refrained from saying, "I told you so," or pointing out the obvious. Carmen not only learned that when you are very hot and thirsty, your stomach needs time to absorb sweet liquids or you will throw up; she also learned she had a pretty smart dad, so maybe it would be smart to listen to him next time.

Some natural consequences are too unsafe, too inconvenient, or too costly to allow. Others might happen too far in the future or be too far removed from the behavior for the child to see the connection. We don't want to use the natural consequence of cavities to teach our kids to brush their teeth. We can't use the natural consequence of smallpox to teach our kids that vaccinations are important. Those are too unsafe. When a natural consequence won't work, we can use a logical consequence. A logical consequence doesn't happen naturally, but is related to the behavior we are trying to change. We wouldn't use the natural consequence of vitamin deficiency to teach our kids to eat their vegetables. However, we might use the logical consequence of no dessert if they don't eat their vegetables.

Think of some repeated arguments you have with your child that have safe and acceptable natural consequences:

_____

_____

_____

_____

If the natural consequence is not acceptable for any reason, we move to logical consequences. We can't prove to our kids that eating vegetables will help them grow up big and strong; the natural consequence is just too far removed from the behavior. So we use a logical consequence and tell them that eating their vegetables is what allows them to eat dessert. Stepping on and breaking a laptop that a child leaves on the floor is too expensive as a consequence. We might say that the logical consequence of leaving things on the floor is to only use the laptop at the dining room table or that they have to ask permission to use it. If a child continues to eat in their room after we've told them not to, it's too inconvenient for us to wait for the natural consequence of the smell of spoiled food (or mice in the house!). But we can say that the logical consequence of leaving food in their room is that we have the right to look for leftover food in their rooms at any time, so they lose the right to privacy.

Natural consequences are what would happen if nobody stepped in: If you don't pick up your toys, they get stepped on and/or broken. If you dawdle in the morning, you won't have time for breakfast, and you will be hungry until lunch. If you use a paintbrush without cleaning it, it will harden and becomes unusable. Logical consequences are used when natural consequences are too dangerous, too costly, or too distant, but logical consequences are still directly related to the behavior: If I have to pick up your toys, you have to do one of my chores to earn them back. If you dawdle in the morning, instead of pancakes and bacon, you get a granola bar. If you use a paintbrush without cleaning it, you can't use my paintbrushes.

It can take some time to find a logical consequence that is safe, age-appropriate, and effective.

Think of some logical consequences for these situations:

Your four-year-old child won't stay near you when you are in a store:

_____

_____

_____

_____

Your fourth grader plays games instead of doing homework:

_____

_____

_____

Your seventeen-year-old doesn't put gas in the car after borrowing it:

_____

_____

_____

_____

For a four-year-old who won't stay near a parent in a crowded store, some logical consequences might be that they have to keep one hand on the cart, that they have to ride in the cart, or even that you have to leave the store early. A logical consequence for a fourth grader who plays games instead of doing homework is that the game console is put away until homework is done. A logical consequence for a seventeen-year-old who doesn't put gas in the car is that the money for gas is doubled and taken out of their allowance.

Since both natural and logical consequences can feel like punishments, it is helpful to present them in a way that is respectful and empathetic.

> Corrine was a foster parent: Her family was welcoming a twelve-year-old boy, Zain, into their home. Corrine had prepared a nice spaghetti dinner. Zain was having trouble eating his spaghetti and was embarrassed. Part way through the meal, Zain threw his plate of spaghetti across the room. Corrine told him, "I cooked a meal that was difficult to eat. It makes sense that you'd feel frustrated and maybe even embarrassed. I'm going to help you out. I'm going to make you a peanut butter sandwich, and let you eat it alone in your room. When you are feeling safer and more comfortable, please come back and join us. If that's too difficult, and you feel safer in your room, I will come see how you are doing after dinner. I'll let you clean up the spaghetti when just you and I are in the room, so you don't have to feel like people are watching and judging you." How different that is from yelling, "Clean that up right now! You only get a peanut butter sandwich, and go to your room until you are ready to come out!" Zain still had consequences for his behavior—he still had to clean up the spaghetti he threw—but Corrine didn't expect him to have a skill he hadn't been taught. She reflected on the situation, acknowledged his feelings, and set logical consequences. She respected his struggle and used his mistake as a teaching tool.

Often the natural or logical consequence is the same as the punishment would be. The difference is in the presentation of the consequence and the relationship between the parent and child. Consequences are presented with empathy and respect. They are presented as a helpful intervention. If they are presented empathetically and respectfully, and as a helpful intervention, your child is more likely to look at you as an ally than an enemy.

> John's sixteen-year-old daughter, Christine, was supposed to come home right after practice. Instead, she drove to Red Robin with her friends. John was quite upset. The logical consequence was that Christine would lose driving privileges for a while. Instead or presenting it as a punishment, John presented it as a logical consequence. Christine didn't get out of practice, but John did have to drive her to practice for a week. However, he didn't drive her to the movies or friends' houses.

During the car rides, Christine shared with her dad some of the struggles she was having in school and with friends. Not only did the logical consequence link to Christine's behavior, but she was actually showing that she needed more time with, and more guidance from, her dad. If John had treated it like a punishment, Christine probably wouldn't have opened up to him on those car rides.

Think about some times when, as a child, you really needed guidance rather than punishment:

_____

_____

_____

_____

Think about some limits you may have needed as a child, even though you fought against them:

_____

_____

_____

_____

Lorena's daughter, Meggan, was a cheerful, happy child who got straight As in school and helped around the house. Then Meggan started seventh grade. Meggan began hanging out with friends who had a bad reputation. She became more argumentative and rebellious at home. She started seeing a boy. Lorena saw that Meggan's boyfriend was somewhat pushy and controlling. One day, Lorena discovered that Meggan was at the park when she said she was at the frozen yogurt shop. Meggan came home with a hickey on her neck. Lorena found texts showing that the boyfriend was pressuring Meggan into sexual activity. Lorena told Meggan she had found the text messages, and because Meggan had been using her phone inappropriately, she lost her phone for a week. Meggan gave her mom her phone, tablet, and laptop. After a week, Lorena still allowed Meggan to go to the frozen yogurt shop, but she told her she was installing a tracker on her phone. Meggan, surprisingly, didn't complain much about all this. She did shout, "You don't trust me!" but Lorena held her ground without arguing back. After a few days, Lorena noticed less stress from Meggan. She realized Meggan had been asking for firmer limits—limits she felt unable, because of peer pressure, to set herself. Meggan's grades improved, and she dropped the boyfriend. Meggan had been in over her head, struggling with issues she wasn't mature enough to handle. The limits and logical consequences allowed Meggan to make better decisions.

When you don't know the most appropriate or helpful logical consequence, that's okay. One of the best things you can do is to admit it. You can say to your child, "I don't know yet what I'm going to do about that." Taking time to think about what the most appropriate logical consequence is has some major benefits:

It gives you time to process and come up with the best consequence and response.

When kids misbehave, often parents overreact with unreasonable, excessive, or difficult consequences. In frustration, we reactively yell, "You're grounded for life!" Or even, "You are grounded for a week!" forgetting about the important event scheduled for that week, or that after day three, we will be tired of them walking around the house with a chip on their shoulder. In the moment, we can forget about the practicalities of the consequences we impose. And then we are stuck. If we stop and think—waiting to impose a consequence—it gives us time to find a consequence that is reasonable and effective.

It shows, if someone is angry, frustrated, or just simply doesn't know what to do, it is a really good idea to stop and think for a while.

We constantly tell our children to do stop and think about their behavior. We tell them to count to ten when they are angry. We ask what they were thinking when they make a rash decision. We say, "What did you think would happen?" when they suffer the consequences of their own behavior. Taking time to think about the logical consequence models the importance of thinking before you act. It shows your kids that you, too, get frustrated but know better than to make an important decision before taking the time to think about it.

It allows your child to feel the apprehension to reflect on what the consequence might be.

Consequences that come too quickly don't allow our kids to reflect on their own behavior. With time to think, they will wonder what consequence you will come up with and what consequence is reasonable. You can even ask your child to think about what the appropriate consequence should be while they wait. (Some children will actually come up with surprisingly fair consequences.) Waiting gives them the time to think about the consequence, and time to consider what they could have done differently in the first place. An immediate response does not give your child the any time to reflect.

Think about an excessive punishment you imposed that you wish you hadn't:

_____

_____

_____

_____

Shorter consequences work better than long, drawn-out consequences. If you tell a teen you are taking her phone away for half an hour, she will spend that half hour thinking about what she did to lose the phone and what she has to do to get it back. If she repeats the behavior that caused her to lose her phone, because you've given it back, you can take it away again for another half hour. Taking her phone away many times for short periods will teach her more quickly than taking it away once for a long time. Children learn through repetition. If you tell her you are taking away her phone for a week, she might spend a little time thinking about her behavior, but will probably spend the majority of the rest of the week thinking about how unfair it is.

To limit misbehavior, you can also simply not to allow your child to get into a situation where they might get into trouble. This can be as simple as taking a sharp knife away from a small child or taking the car keys away from a teenager. It can be taking the gaming system with you instead of telling your child they can't play video games while you are at work. It can be keeping treats in a high cupboard that your kids can't reach, or not buying sweets. Or you can plan for situations that tend to be difficult for your child. That can be putting a toy in each of your toddler's hands so they aren't tempted to touch things when you will be somewhere that isn't "child proofed." It can be bringing a book or quiet toy for them to the doctor's office or church. It can be moving the hamper into the bathroom to help them remember to put their dirty clothes in the hamper instead of on the floor.

Lynn's young son, Mogie, slept in pull-ups. In the morning, he would climb out of his toddler bed and climb up on the couch, getting the couch wet, before Lynn could change him. Mogie was just too young to understand why he shouldn't sit on the couch. Instead of trying to teach her son not to sit on the couch when he was wet, Lynn simply put a towel on the couch in the morning. Tossing the towel in the washing machine was much easier than trying to clean the couch every day. And instead of starting every day frustrated, they started each day more calmly. There would be plenty of time for Mogie to learn this lesson when he was old enough.

6
Problem Solving
I came here for an argument

"You can't win an argument."

—Dale Carnegie

If nothing seems to be working, and the problem is ongoing, it's time to have a longer conversation with your child. Set a time that is good for both of you. Give your child a chance to talk about their behavior without interrupting them. Simply let them express themselves without judging or arguing. Then you get to talk about your concerns without your child interrupting or arguing. If the problem is not turning in homework, your child might say they forgot, it's too hard, or they don't see why it is important. Then you might say you want them to succeed, and it's frustrating to you that they don't turn in their homework. Practice listening to each other with full attention and reflective comments.

After both of you have had your say, start to brainstorm. Write down every idea you can think of—even if the idea is unreasonable or unfair. You can even start with some silly solutions. If a child isn't doing their homework, you can suggest eliminating all homework. It's okay that some of these ideas are unworkable. Brainstorming is about being creative and exploring all ideas. Sometimes a ridiculous idea will lead to a reasonable idea, and sometimes an unworkable idea will lead to a workable one.

After you have made a long list, go through it together and cross out all the silly or unacceptable ideas. Then you both circle your favorite ideas. Next, have an open conversation about which of the ideas you'd both like to try. Or, if you can, adjust one of those ideas or combine two of them. Make an agreement and set a time to meet again to see if the solution is working. If it isn't, start the problem-solving process over again. This is time-consuming, but it is less time-consuming than constant or repeated arguments.

Steps to problem-solving an ongoing issue:

1. Set a time that is good for the parent and the child.

2. Allow the child to talk fully about their point of view without interruption.

3. You, as a parent, get to fully talk about your point of view without interruption.

4. Make a list together, brainstorming possible solutions. It's okay if you don't agree or if some solutions are unrealistic. Just write as many ideas as you can both think of.

5. Together, cross off the ideas you both know are unreasonable or won't work.

6. Together, circle one, two, or three solutions you are both willing to try.

7. Set a time to review and see if the solution you agreed on is working.

You will probably have to use all of these strategies more than once. Probably even more than twice. A friend of mine used to say that parenting is 10 percent intervention and 90 percent repetition. Repetition is not only okay, but it is often the most effective way to instill a lesson. If the consequence is too long, they might think it's not worth behaving well for that long. So many parents complain that they have taken this toy, that electronic device, and that privilege away and they have nothing else to take away! The trick is to take it away, and then give it back. This gives your child chance after chance to earn their toy, electronics, or privilege. And parenting is 90 percent repetition.

There are many alternatives to traditional punishment. Punishment can give you some results, but it has many drawbacks. It leads the child to focus on the punishment rather than the lesson. It creates conflict rather than trust between parent and child. Quick punishment doesn't allow your child time to feel remorse. Model thinking before you take action by taking the time to think about your responses when your child misbehaves. Repeated consequences instill learning. Natural and logical consequences help a child see the connection between their behavior and the result of their behavior, and make it easier for them to understand the reason to change their behavior. Consequences also make it more likely they will take responsibility and make it harder to blame their parents. Remove the temptation to misbehave, explain the reason for following the rules, and set your child up for success.

7

Getting Kids to Help

If I said it once...

"Life is really simple, but we insist on making it complicated."

—Confucius

Parenting is about teaching our kids to stop doing things we don't want them to do, but it is also about encouraging them to do the things we do want them to do. How do we teach our children to do their chores and help out around the house? It can feel like we're constantly reminding them of the simple chores that need to done: "Take your dishes to the sink." "Pick up your clothes." "Take out the garbage." There are ways to motivate our kids to help out without nagging, yelling, or lecturing.

It is rare that our kids jump up to help when we walk through the door with a load of groceries. To get them to help, you can simply say, "I have a load of groceries." If they don't get up to help, you can add your expectations, "I have a load of groceries, one of your jobs is to help put groceries away." You might include your feelings, and say, "I have a load of groceries. You guys are playing games, and I'm starting to feel frustrated."

It might even include future consequences. "I have a load of groceries. If the groceries don't get put away, they will spoil." Or consequences about your own behavior. "I have a load of groceries, the counter is messy, and you guys are playing games. If I have to put all the groceries away by myself, I won't have the energy to drive you to your friend's house tonight." Consequences are different than threats. They naturally flow from the situation and aren't excessive.

Or, you can go the opposite direction, and try a silly joke. "I have a load of groceries, and there's a million dollars in one of these bags. Whoever finds it first, gets to keep it!" Make sure your joke is silly enough that they don't actually believe it. They won't believe a million dollars, but if you say there is $10.00 in one of the bags, they might actually believe you. This is similar to the "giving in fantasy" idea we discussed in Chapter 2 that works when listening to feelings.

Or, you can go even shorter, and just say, "Groceries." "Groceries, kids." "Hey, groceries."

> Dalton was never quite ready to leave the house whenever it was time for him to go to daycare. His mom, Maggie, gave him plenty of warning. She gave him a ten-minute warning. She gave him a five-minute warning. She turned off the television. Invariably, when it was time to go out the door, Dalton's shoes weren't on. Maggie ran around trying to find Dalton's shoes, shoved them on his feet, and spent the ride to daycare lecturing him about his shoes. This didn't teach Dalton time management, responsibility, or consideration for others. What it taught him was that if he didn't do something, his mom would do it for him! He tuned out the lecture on the way to school, looking out the window. He began to think of his mom as someone who yelled all the time. After taking a parenting class, Maggie changed her behavior. She kept an eye on the clock. As she turned off the television, she just said, "Shoes." Nothing more, just "Shoes." Dalton began petting the cat. Maggie said, "Shoes." Dalton said he was hungry. Maggie said, "Shoes." Dalton told his mother she was the "bestest" mom in the world. Maggie said, "Shoes." Dalton finally got his shoes. After several mornings, Maggie only had to say shoes once, maybe twice, before Dalton got his shoes. They spent the drive to daycare talking, telling jokes, and singing with the radio.

Repeating one word regardless of the distractions and diversions your kid uses can work. When it's time to go to bed, you repeat, "Bedtime." Your child might say, "But, Mom, I love you, and just want to be with you." You say, "Bedtime." Then your child says, "But Johnny gets to stay up later!" You say, "Bedtime." Then your child might say, "You're the meanest mom in the world!" and you say, "Bedtime." Then your child says, "I forgot, I was supposed to bring cupcakes to school tomorrow," and you say, "Bedtime."

Saying one word is about redirecting and refocusing your child. Regardless of how many times you repeat yourself, giving in at the end just teaches your child to ignore you a little longer, to distract you a little more, and to complain a little bit louder next time. Instead of giving in, apply a logical consequence, or tell your child you are going to take the time to think about a logical consequence.

You can also offer your child a choice. If your child refuses to get dressed for school, you can say, "You can wear the blue shirt or the green shirt." This will work better than saying, "You have to get dressed."

Many people misunderstand the concept of giving choices. Offering a choice isn't about allowing your child to decide if they are going to do something or not; offering a choice is allowing them to decide how they will do it. Saying, "You can eat your vegetables or skip dessert" is not what the concept of giving a choice is about. Saying, "You can eat your peas first or your carrots," or saying, "You can put butter and salt on your peas or eat them plain," or even, "You can eat three bites, five bites, or seven bites of your peas," is offering a choice. Offering a choice often reroutes situations that would have turned into power struggles. Feeling powerful about some part of complying frees the child up to comply.

Simply asking children to do a task is also an option. However, asking suggests that they can say no. If we don't give them a chance to say no, we avoid a power struggle. Stating facts, consequences, and feelings, repeating a word, and giving choices help children choose a path of helpfulness, while minimizing arguments.

8
Motivation

But why?

"Many of life's failures are people who did not realize how close
they were to success when they gave up."

—Thomas A. Edison

When our child isn't doing what we want or expect them to do, we are quick to jump to the conclusion that they don't want to do it. But they might not know it needs to be done. They might not know why it needs to be done. They might not know they are expected to do it. They might not know how to do it. They might not know how to do it well. And sometimes, they just haven't practiced doing it enough.

Sometimes kids truly do not know that something needs to be done. Simply pointing out that the garbage needs to be out by the curb before eight o'clock in the morning or it won't get picked up might help them actually take the garbage to the curb.

They might not know they are expected to do it.

> When Debbie began playing tennis, she assumed that since there was a line down the center of the court, the person on the right side of the court was supposed to hit the balls that bounced on the right side of the court, and the person on the left side of the court was supposed to hit the balls that bounced on the left side of the court. Because Debbie didn't know either person could hit balls on other side of the court, her partners got frustrated with her, and thought she was lazy or unmotivated. After Debbie played for a while, her coach told her if her partner moved to the left to hit a ball, she should move over to cover more of the court. All it took was someone explaining the expectations to Debbie to get her to change her behavior.

Making your explanations clear, with specific instructions, will help your child succeed. Explaining to your child the purpose behind your expectations will make them more likely to comply.

List some chores your child may not fully understand how to do:

_____

_____

_____

_____

Another way to limit problem behavior is to take action that makes problem behavior unlikely. Instead of explaining to a young child why knives are dangerous, simply take the knife away. If you have a toddler, don't keep breakable items on the coffee table. Instead of taking your young child to the tempting toy aisle to pick out a birthday present for a friend—a sure recipe for a temper tantrum—give the child a couple of choices; then pick out the toy yourself. If your child tends to forget to take their coat to school, hang the coat on the front doorknob. Set your child up for success instead of creating situations that make it is easy for them to disobey.

Darren's son, Noah, was supposed to bring in the garbage can on trash day. Noah was a daydreamer. He would walk right past the garbage can without noticing it. He wasn't purposefully defying his father; he just hadn't yet developed the habit of dragging in the trash can. When Darren got home from work and saw that the trash can was still at the side of the road, he would yell at Noah to go bring it in. Noah would, but it was an unpleasant weekly practice for both Darren and Noah. Instead of continuing a pattern that clearly wasn't working, Darren attached a bright red hat to the garbage can. Noah may have easily daydreamed his way past the trash can, but not when the trash can had a hat on it! After a few months, Noah developed the habit of noticing the trash can, and the hat was no longer necessary.

Parents sometimes inadvertently set their kids up for misbehavior. Don't ask your child with chocolate all over their face if they got into the cookie jar. You know they got into the cookie jar. Asking them tempts them to lie or defend themselves. Say, "I see you got in the cookie jar," instead. Don't ask your child if they have homework, ask, "What homework do you have?" Asking if they have homework makes it easy for them to disregard or deny the homework they have. Making it easy for a child to behave works better than making it easy for them to disobey.

"Seek opportunities to show you care.
The smallest gestures often make the biggest difference."

—John Wooden

9

Praise

Treat your children well

"The cost of praising someone is nil—but every psychological study shows the payoff is huge."

—Harvey Mackay

Parenting is more than responding to bad behavior. It is also responding to good behavior. Shouldn't we spend as much time working on our response to good behavior? Studies show that children (and adults) respond more favorably to praise than punishment. Positive reinforcement is the most effective way to get your child to repeat behavior. Praise can nourish and preserve your relationship with your child.

"Most people do not receive nearly enough appreciation. How can this be when appreciation is free, easy, and readily available? All you have to do is speak. Go give some away now."

—Roberta Shaler

When our children does something we like, we want to praise them in a way that encourages them to do it again. We want praise they can internalize. We want praise to help them see the values underpinning their behavior. We want praise to make them feel proud, and to make us feel proud of the child we send out into the world.

"We must return optimism to our parenting. To focus on the joys, not the hassles; the love, not the disappointments; the common sense, not the complexities."

—Fred G. Gosman

Praise is just as important as consequences. Although sometimes praise comes naturally, it may take time to come up with sincere, specific praise. Almost anything a young child does can be immediately (and sometimes irritatingly) reinforced by praise as simple as smiling or clapping. When a baby smiles, their parents smile back and engage more with the baby. Then the baby smiles more. When a baby waves "bye bye" for the first time, their parents say, "Yay," and clap their hands. The baby smiles and waves "bye bye" again. A toddler will do something and look at adults, waiting for their approval in a smile. When school-aged children tell jokes and people laugh, they tell the joke again, expecting laughter—then they tell it again. It only takes one success for them to repeat the behavior.

There are some specific ways to praise that work well.

Have you ever had someone praise you by saying, "Wow, you look good today!" It makes you wonder how you looked yesterday. Have you ever had someone praise you by telling you something you know isn't true? "This is the best chocolate cake ever!" Do you believe them? Praise that we don't believe can make us distrustful, rather than encourage us. If someone says, "Great job!" you wonder what was so great about it.

> Olivia knew she wasn't the best singer in her glee club. At one point, while learning a difficult song, she asked a better singer to help her. After singing, Olivia asked if she got all the notes right. The other singer said, "You did better, and you were quick to find the right note if you didn't hit it at first." That was more helpful than an insincere and vague, "You did great!" or a critical, "You didn't hit the right notes." It was also better than an insincere and unhelpful, "Yes, you got all the notes right." She learned to trust and take the advice of the singer who helped her because her praise was positive, sincere, and accurate.

Repeated or exaggerated praise begins to sound insincere and loses its effectiveness. When someone praises us insincerely, we question their motives. Insincere praise might make us think the other person is trying to get something from us, rather than give something to us. It might lead us to distrust the person praising us. It might also lead us to distrust our own self-evaluation.

Think of some times when someone praised you but you felt it was insincere:

_____

_____

_____

_____

One dilemma in schools is about merit-based awards versus participation awards. While it is nice to be inclusive, if every child gets an award, they begin to lose their value. Studies have shown that children actually work harder for merit-based rewards. There is a way to include all children, while also being sincere.

> Jessa played tennis in high school. At the end of the school year, her coach gave every team member an award. Since every team member couldn't possibly be the "most valuable player," the coach took care that the awards were personal, accurate, and sincere. She did give awards for "best singles player" and "most wins" but also gave awards for "most improved," "most spirited," "best sportsmanship," etc. Because the awards were sincere and truly reflected the qualities of each player, they were all accepted with graciousness and pleasure. Jessa knew she wasn't the best player, but she knew she had great team spirit. Winning "most spirited" clearly showed that her coach noticed and valued her contribution to the team.

Two very simple ways exist to make praise accurate and believable. You can simply say what happened. A baby smiles and we naturally say, "There's that smile." When a toddler uses the potty, we say, "You used the potty!" If the child takes out the trash the first time we remind them, we say, "You took out the trash after one reminder." If a teenager comes home before curfew, we say, "You came home before curfew." Be a mirror that reflects what happened and add positive emotion or descriptive word.

If you are trying to reinforce a particular quality, you can add a descriptive word. "You got an A. That's commitment." "You took out the trash after one reminder. I'm pleased." "You came home before curfew. I'm relieved. Thank you for being considerate."

> In high school, Miguel always got good grades on his papers. One time, he thought his paper was not up to his usual standards, but he still got an A. He wondered if the teacher actually read his papers. The next paper he wrote, he purposefully made glaring mistakes. He got an A. His grades became unhelpful because they weren't an accurate reflection of his work. He began putting jokes or inappropriate comments in his papers. Miguel could have been learning, but his high grades did not help him nearly as much as accuracy would have.

The most effective praise is an honest reflection of what you feel or what you see. If someone bakes a chocolate cake that you are enjoying, you can say, "I'm loving this chocolate cake." If someone writes an excellent paper, you can say, "I read your paper; it was easy to follow, you incorporated ideas from your research, and you gave a clear summary at the end." You can certainly add more general words of praise: "I'm loving this chocolate cake. You're a great cook!" or "Your paper was easy to follow. Great job!"

Simply reflecting what you saw them do is a great way to praise your child. Saying, "You were stuck on that level for five days, and you kept going back to it," will remind a child of their determination. Adding, "That takes determination!" isn't always necessary, but can strengthen the praise. Also, adding how you feel can strengthen the praise. "You were stuck on level five for days, and you kept going back to it. That takes determination! And I felt proud."

The closer praise is to a specific behavior, the more effective it is. When we tell dogs to sit, we give them treats right after they do so, not two hours later. Children have longer memories, but several benefits exist to praising them immediately after an event: It's easier to be specific and sincere, it increases the chances the child will learn, and it shows the child you are attentive to them.

"You must reward the kind of behavior that you want."

—James Mattis

Numerous studies show that repeated positive reinforcement works better than repeated punishment in changing behavior. If you truly want your children to do something differently, catch them doing it correctly, and praise them. Or catch them doing something where they display similar skills or qualities, and praise that. If you want them to be responsible for doing their homework even when it is difficult, praise them for being persistent enough to get through a difficult level of a game they are playing. Remind them of their determination to work through difficult problems, even when they get frustrated. After you praise them several times for being determined and not giving up when playing video games, next time they get frustrated with their homework, acknowledge their feelings of frustration, and remind them very honestly that you believe they have the determination to do it. They'll believe you because you've told them so before.

You can actually create events to elicit praise-worthy behavior.

> Yesenia, a ten-year-old, was very shy and did not like to talk in front of people. Because she rarely did so, her parents had little opportunity to praise her for talking to others. So, they thought of every example of times she interacted instead of being shy and praised her for specific examples. They reminded her of the time she said "Trick or treat" by herself. They reminded her of the time she explained her science fair project to strangers. They simply repeated to her what they saw, and added statements like, "That shows bravery," or "I was impressed when I saw you give that speech." Yesenia's confidence grew, and she felt more comfortable interacting with others.

"Instruction does much, but encouragement everything."
—Johann Wolfgang von Goethe

Praise is also a way to encourage your child to follow their dreams and try new things. If your five-year-old daughter dreams of being a ballerina, you can praise her grace, athleticism, and persistence. You can give her opportunities to practice those attributes, whether by enrolling her in dancing classes or simply watching her twirl in the living room. She will better develop the skills you praise whether or not she becomes a ballerina. If your ten-year-old son daydreams of beating up the school bully, you can praise him for his sense of justice and his bravery. You can talk to him about people you admire who have found ways other than violence to pursue justice and show bravery. He will value justice and bravery, even as he finds a different way to respond to a bully.

> Jordan was fourteen when she told her parents that at eighteen she planned to move to New York to become an actress. Instead of focusing on the dangers of such a move, Jordan's mother first praised her enthusiasm and independence. Then they spent countless hours researching what it took to live in New York. Instead of thinking her mother was dismissing her dream, Jordan felt encouraged and supported. That allowed Jordan the freedom to explore her dream in a practical way, and decide whether or not moving to New York was truly what she wanted to do.

"Kindness in words creates confidence. Kindness in thinking creates profoundness. Kindness in giving creates love."
—Lao Tzu

Our goal isn't to have our children's behavior dependent on rewards, just as our goal isn't to have our children's behavior dependent on fear of punishment. We want our children to do the right thing because they believe it's the right thing to do. As you praise your child, you will see their good actions become habits. Habits result when the child has internalized the message and behavior. Once they internalize the behavior, it is not as necessary to praise them for that particular activity. But be sure to offer praise for the behavior once in a while to ensure it continues, and to show your appreciation.

10

Structure

Rock the boat

"Free the child's potential, and you will transform him into the world."
—Maria Montessori

Many discoveries are made when people are looking for something completely different. The concept of the "big bang" was discovered because two astronomers found unexplained static while working on unrelated research. Penicillin was discovered when Alexander Fleming returned from a vacation to find a "strange fungus" growing on cultures he had been working on; today, penicillin is called a discovery made from dirty dishes. Chocolate chip cookies were invented by a baker trying to make chocolate cookies. She thought chunks of chocolate would melt and spread evenly through the cookies.

In one study, social scientists recorded play patterns of children in a public park for one year. About halfway through the year, a fence was built around the park and they noticed that the children's play patterns changed. Before the fence, most of the children played toward the center of the park, with one or two daring to get close to the perimeter. After the fence was built, the children spread out and used more of the park. The fence made the children feel safer to use more of the area.

When we have no boundaries, most of us limit ourselves more than we have to, while some of us push past what is safe. When there are appropriate boundaries, we can stay safe and also have more freedom—boundaries increase freedom *and* safety. Traffic rules allow us to drive more safely. An open intersection on a busy street would be chaos and unsafe without rules. Allowing our children to make mistakes does not mean we ignore rules and boundaries. As parents, we want to make sure the mistakes our children make are not dangerous or damaging.

Even though children complain about boundaries, they need them. If children are allowed to eat whatever they want, with no constraints, they will eat unhealthy foods for a while, but eventually, without intervention, they will begin to crave and eat healthier foods. Children constantly test to ensure they have safe but flexible boundaries. While this can be frustrating, if parents look at these tests for what they are—reassurances of safety—they become less frustrating. We have all seen a toddler cry, then look to see if anyone is watching. The toddler is not being manipulative; they are reassuring themselves that if they *do* cry, someone will pay attention. Most of us have examples of times our child blatantly misbehaved, ensuring they would be caught. Sometimes children act out because they need the reassurance of the "fence"—the rules and boundaries adults provide.

As a counseling intern, I often observed and assisted in elementary school classrooms. The teacher's time-out area was a square marked off by masking tape with nothing in it but pillows. Children could be sent, or elect to go, to time-out. Every Monday, before noon, Jordan was either sent or elected to go to time-out. Trying to be a helpful behavioral assistant, I identified this as a problem and talked to the teacher about how we could get Jordan to avoid time-out. The experienced teacher explained to me that the time-outs were necessary for Jordan to feel safe enough to focus at school. Jordan had a very chaotic home life. School provided safety and structure. Monday through Friday, Jordan had structure and he knew what to expect. Over the weekend, his chaotic home was a frightening place for him. He knew school was safe, but he needed to be reminded, so every Monday, through his behavior, he asked, "Is school still a safe and predictable place?" And every Monday, by going or being sent to time-out when he misbehaved, he got the answer. "Yes, school is still a safe and predictable place." Going to time-out every Monday was not the problem—it was the solution.

Jordan's story is another reminder of the difference between discipline and punishment. The teacher made time-out a reminder of boundaries. It was not shameful, wrong, or mean; it was to help the child learn and shape their own behavior.

Adults double-check that the doors are locked at night for reassurance. We double-check, and sometimes triple-check, that our wallets are in our pockets when we leave the house and that our passports are in our carry-ons when we travel. I knew a woman who began packing her curling iron in her car because she was always worried that she had left it plugged in! Kids need reassurance, too.

Name some things you do to reassure yourself of something you already know:

_____

_____

_____

_____

A child asking for reassurance can feel repetitive and maybe even frustrating, but it helps the child feel safe and secure. Allow your child to do that. What are some ways you think your child misbehaves that might actually be a way they are asking for reassurance?

_____

_____

_____

_____

There are two types of buildings that fall over during an earthquake: rickety, wobbly, unstable buildings and older, brick buildings that don't bend at all. If you look at videos of tall buildings during an earthquake, you will see that they sway. They have sturdy internal structure, but they also have a bit of flexibility. This is also true of highways and bridges. Built of concrete and steel, made to hold tons of weight, they are extremely strong structures, but without the ability to sway, they would not withstand an earthquake. Being a safe parent is like being a safe building during an earthquake. We can't be so unstable that we topple at the first strong wind. Neither can we be so inflexible that we don't bend in a storm. Sometimes children push on the building to make sure it is stable but with just a little bit of sway. Sometimes our children misbehave because they need to feel safe. They need a reminder that you are stable but also flexible.

> Melody loved stickers. Her dad, Gage, would find stickers on the walls, on the refrigerator, and once on the cat. Instead of telling her she couldn't put stickers anywhere, Gage and Melody picked one piece of furniture, her hand-me-down dresser, that she was allowed to put as many stickers on as she pleased—but only on that dresser. Melody's dresser was covered in stickers, but the rest of the house was sticker-free.

Parents are the buildings. Children are the "earthquake safety inspectors." At times, children will misbehave specifically (if not consciously) to test our structural integrity. When your child doesn't want to go to bed at their bedtime, they may be asking for a reminder of your structure. When your child asks for candy before dinner when they know better, they may be asking for a reminder of safe boundaries. When your teenager gets home five minutes after curfew, they may be asking for reminders of safe, but flexible, boundaries.

Flexibility, as well as structure, is important. We don't want our parenting to be like an unyielding brick and mortar building that can't withstand an earthquake. Setting school-night bedtimes for our children, but allowing them to stay up a bit later on the weekends, is an example of flexibility.

List some examples of flexibility in stable rules in your family:

_____

_____

_____

_____

List some general rules you allow your child to disregard every once in a while:

_____

_____

_____

_____

Some examples might be allowing your child to have a later bedtime on weekends or allowing them to skip chores on their birthday. Flexibility can be allowing your child to stay up until midnight on New Year's

Eve. Flexibility is having pancakes for dinner every once in a while. These examples show flexibility, but they do not threaten stability or consistency.

Consistency is absolutely important in parenting, but flexibility does not need to undermine consistency. Studies show that if something is done about 70 percent of the time, we think of it as consistent. When people think of their childhood, they think there was *always* milk in the fridge, though there probably wasn't always milk in the fridge; they think they *always* went to church on Sundays, though they may only have gone *most* Sundays. As an adult, we say we *always* make our beds, though we probably don't.

What are some things you have internalized as consistent that don't happen 100 percent of the time?

_____

_____

_____

_____

Consistency is important in parenting, but consistency does not mean perfection. Sometimes, we are tired, we have had a long day, or it is a special occasion. It is okay to overlook the half-done chores, or to allow dessert even though half the vegetables are still on the plate. Kids feel safest when there are consistent boundaries, but those boundaries need to have just a little bit of flexibility.

Structure is not inflexible and rigid, nor is it lenient and indulgent. Think of the structure you provide your child that is firm yet flexible, stable yet receptive, definite yet accommodating. Structure provides safety from harm, but it also provides safety to grow. Structure is essential and increases freedom and fun. Flexibility is essential and does not undermine structure, and it also increases safety and fun.

11

Development

What's the lesson, here?

*"One thing I had learned from watching chimpanzees with
their infants is that having a child should be fun."*

—Jane Goodall

As children grow, they move through developmental stages. Each stage has its challenges and its goals. Recognizing what your child is learning at each stage may help you to understand their behavior. It can help you to apply appropriate natural or logical consequences, and it can also help you guide them through the given stage with minimal discomfort for all involved. It may even allow you to enjoy each stage!

Most behaviors we find irritating are behaviors that are helping a child learn a new skill or concept. They are irritating because they are repetitive. But they are important because your child is learning something. If we recognize the reason behind the behavior, instead of irritating, it can become fun.

Dan's five year old daughter, Katie, would yell, "No!" every night when he told her it was bedtime. Sometimes, she would hide behind the couch. Dan realized Katie usually needed more time to transition from one activity to another than he was allowing her. So he acknowledged her feelings and helped her transition in a fun way. At bedtime, Dan and Katie would sing the "I don't want to go to bed" song. Ten minutes of singing helped her make the transition. It took less time, and was more fun, and it worked better than arguing every night.

We've all had the experience of a child pushing something off the highchair tray. We pick it up. The child pushes it off again. We pick it up, etc. This is not the child trying to frustrate us, and it is not the child being manipulative. This is the age when the child's awareness moves from random events to cause and effect. They are learning that behavior has consequences. Before this age, their world was random. Randomly, their bottom felt wet and uncomfortable. Crying had nothing to do with their parent coming. Events were not related to each other. Now, they are learning the world is, in fact, not random. They can affect it. When they push something, it falls to the ground. They are fascinated. *Will it fall this time?* They wonder. *Why, yes, it does!* They are so fascinated by this epiphany that they do it again and again—they play with this concept to learn it.

The first time a baby learns to clap, they do it over and over again. The first time they dress themselves, they try on every outfit in the room. The first time they learn to make macaroni and cheese out of the box, they want to make it every night. Do you remember first learning to drive? You probably wanted to drive all the time: "Do we need milk at the store? I'll go pick it up!" "Shouldn't you return that casserole dish to Aunt Caroline? Let me drive it over to her house!" At every age, for every skill they learn, children have to practice. Many of the repetitive behaviors parents find irritating or believe to be manipulative are the child practicing a new skill or concept.

> Sherry and her one-year-old daughter, Gabby, were on the tennis court. Sherry handed Gabby a tennis ball. Gabby said, "Thank you." Then Sherry said, "Please," and Gabby handed the ball back. Sherry said, "Thank you." Sherry and Gabby repeated this over and over. For Gabby, it was a new delight every time she got the tennis ball; and a new delight every time she handed it back. Mother and daughter had made learning to say, "Please" and "Thank you" fun.

We want our children to learn consequences. We want them to understand cause and effect. If we punish or stop these behaviors, we take away the chance for our child to learn an important lesson. Responding like a teacher helps. Looking at behavior as a developmental milestones makes them fun rather than irritating.

What do you guess your child is learning in the following common behaviors?

Playing peek-a-boo:

_____

_____

_____

_____

Throwing a temper tantrum:

_____

_____

_____

_____

Emptying out an entire tube of toothpaste:

_____

_____

_____

Children are fascinated with peak-a-boo. Before six months of age, if you hid something behind your back, your child thought it no longer existed. At about six months, kids realize things exist even if they can't see them. As they are learning that things still exist even if they are hidden; peek-a-boo becomes a magic trick for them. Their parent's face disappears, and then reappears as if by magic. They are surprised and delighted every time their parent's face disappears and then "magically" reappears.

Why is it important to believe that things exist even if you can't see them?

When children throw temper tantrums, they are learning independence. Before the age of about two, a child has no concept of separation from other people. They believe everyone feels what they feel. After they learn they are separate individuals, they realize they can think and feel things that others don't. Independence from others is an important lesson.

Why is it important for a child to learn that they can feel very differently than those around them?

Emptying out an entire tube of toothpaste, taking all the pots and pans out of the cupboards, pulling all your shirts out of your drawer is a child's way of exploring their world. Exploring the world is an experience we want our children to have. We want them to look beyond themselves, to question, to wonder, to investigate.

Instead of looking at your child's repetitive behavior as irritating, try to think about the lesson they are struggling with. Try to find a fun and productive way to for them to learn that lesson.

"There are only two lasting bequests we can hope to give our children.
One of these is roots, the other, wings."
—Johann Wolfgang von Goethe

A Final Note

Reading a book on parenting is much easier than parenting. Applying what you've read and learned is challenging. It is a challenge to set aside (or throw away) old and familiar parenting practices and begin using new and uncomfortable ideas, but it is an investment in, and a promise to, your children. Learning new concepts, hearing examples, and thinking and writing about the kind of parent you want to be can fill you with inspiration. But then your child is standing in front of you whining, "It's not fair," or "I didn't do it," or "Why do I have to...?" You are frustrated; you are busy. It's challenging to apply what you've learned to that cranky and misbehaving child in front of you. They will make mistakes. You will make mistakes. As we have learned, that is okay. Not only is it okay, but your own mistakes can become learning moments for both you and your child.

A big part of parenting is simply listening—listening to feelings, creating a space for your child to share their feelings, allowing them to come to their own understanding of the problem and design their own solution. Another big part of parenting is standing back and allowing your child to make their own mistakes and learn from those mistakes, so they can avoid such mistakes in the future. Whether it's consequences or praise, often one simple word or a simple description is what a child will internalize. Sometimes these simple solutions are difficult to apply, and we want to jump in too soon and too often. But, like teaching our child to ride a bike, often, our job is to stand back and be ready with hugs, wisdom, and bandages, and let them fall.

Parenting truly is one of the hardest jobs in the world, but it can also be the most fulfilling. It can be the most enjoyable experience you will ever have. Have the confidence to apply what you've learned and improve the lives of your children and your whole family—maybe even the world.

I challenge you to make and keep this commitment to your children. Listen to feelings, and empathize with your child. Allow your children to make mistakes so they can learn from them. Apply discipline like a teacher. Set boundaries and limits with clarity and purpose; expect your child to be responsible. Be accurate and reflective in your praise, so your child learns to internalize praise. Set a goal to use what you've learned, and learn from your mistakes. You will see improvement in yourself and in your child.

About the Author

Besides being a parent, I have been a mental health counselor with a child and family emphasis for more than twenty years. I have developed and taught more parenting classes than I can recall. I've worked with parents who find themselves doing things their parents did—things they hated and promised never to do when they had kids of their own. Few things are more satisfying than meeting a parent who is at their wits' end, and helping them learn how to guide their children into becoming happy, successful, and kind adults. Great joy comes from guiding parents from exhaustion, frustration, and confusion to confidence, skillfulness, and wisdom.

This transformation takes time and effort. Being a parent truly is one of the most difficult jobs in the world. It is astonishing how much influence we have over our children. Being thrust into parenthood with very little training, and usually very little experience, can be scary and overwhelming. The love we have for our children is what motivates us to become better parents. I wish that was enough, but we also need information, skill, and practice to raise healthy children.

"'To love' is an active verb."

—Ogden Nash

Contact the Author

Geralyn Peterson is available for presentations on parenting, emotional intelligence, and other self-help, relationship, and personal growth topics, including

- The Up and Up on Parenting

- Gandhi Got Mad: Using Anger as a Tool

- Setting Yourself Up for Success

- Understanding Anxiety

- Replacing Negative Thoughts with Helpful Ideas

- Storytelling to a New You

Whether your audience is 10 or 10,000, a local school, church, or community group; counseling agency; or large organization, Geralyn Peterson can customize a presentation, training, or consultation for you. Using different teaching styles, examples and exercises, Geralyn makes learning easy and entertaining.

Geralyn is a Washington State approved supervisor for licensed counselors.

Visit Geralyn's website to schedule, discuss, or create your presentation or training.

www.upandupwellness.com